Free Bonus

This book is really just the beginning of your journey. In order to support you in your efforts at growing your tax practice, we created a **membership website** that has additional training and resources to help you build your tax resolution practice.

The great news is that access to this site is 100% free. To get access, go to:

www.TaxMarketingHQ.com/bonus

Here is what you'll receive:

- A comprehensive 6-hour video series that introduces you to the essentials of starting and growing a tax resolution practice, including the fundamentals of marketing, client intake, practice management, sales, and tax resolution case work.
- Detailed training on how to find your first tax resolution client.
- How to quote tax resolution fees.
- The world famous *One-Hour Per Day Marketing Plan*.
- Access to complimentary CE/CPE webinars on IRS Collections topics.
- Additional links, resources, and bonuses from the book.
- A few surprises along the way.

You can access everything at:

https://TaxMarketingHQ.com/bonus

Please note that this offer is subject to change or substitution at any time.

TaxMarketingHQ.com

IMPORTANT NOTICE – PLEASE READ!

While every effort has been taken to ensure that the information contained herein is accurate as of the time of publication, technology is constantly changing. Software, such as WordPress, and online services are changing <u>literally</u> every day. The examples illustrated in this manual were current as of the time of publication, but the specific options, formatting, technical specifications, service pricing, and everything else illustrated in this manual should be <u>expected</u> to change with time. Neither the author or publisher can anticipate these changes. Neither the author or publisher are liable for any changes in technology and information that may be different from what you see explained here. *In other words, use this manual as a guide, but it is your responsibility to adapt the strategies explained herein to any changes in technologies or online services.*

The applicability of the marketing strategies discussed in this book may vary depending upon your skill set, the geographical location of your practice, economic factors, your target market, and other factors that are beyond the control of the author and publisher. Any income examples used in this publication are for illustrative purposes only, and are not a guarantee of income, nor are they necessarily representative of specific tax professionals.

This publication is designed to provide accurate and authoritative information in regards to the subject matter covered, but it is sold with the understanding that the publisher is not engaged in rendering legal or accounting services, and no information contained herein should be construed as legal advice.

If legal advice or other expert assistance is required, the services of a competent professional person should be sought. The publisher does not guarantee or warrant that readers who use the information provided in this publication will achieve results similar to those discussed.

Like all things in life, your results and success in business are directly connected to your own motivation and level of action. The strategies described in this book do work, but they only work if you <u>*take action*</u> to make them work. Nobody else can make you successful, you must take the actions necessary to get there; this manual is just a roadmap.

v1.00
April 19, 2014
Sydney Edition

Table of Contents

Introduction 7
   Firm Web Site vs Lead Generation Web Sites 8
   Some Definitions 8
The Mechanics of Building Lead Generation Sites 11
   Step 1: Keyword research 12
   Step 2: Find a domain name 20
   Step 3: Web hosting 22
   Step 4: Tie domain name to web hosting (Update DNS) 25
   Step 5: Install WordPress. 27
   Step 6: Add a theme to WordPress. 31
   Step 7: Obtain an email autoresponder system. 41
   Step 8: Create follow up emails. 45
   Step 9: Create signup form. 48
   Step 10: Place signup form into WordPress site. 54
   Step 11: Set up blog post broadcaster. 57
   Step 12: Create an editorial schedule. 63
   Step 13: Upload report and add link to email. 66
Traffic Precedes Leads 75
The Pareto SEO Strategy 76
   Things I Don't Do 77
   Be Listed 78
      How Backlinks Work 78
   Be Published 81
      Article Marketing 81
      Guest Blogging 82
      Press Coverage 82
      Video 82
   Be Engaged 83
      Facebook, Twitter, Google+ 84
Paid Traffic 87
   Facebook Ads 87
Resources 92
   Additional Example Lead Generation Sites 92
   Sample Emails 93
   Sample Report 103

Conclusion 107

"Creating Online Tax Client Lead Funnels"

By Jassen Bowman, EA

Introduction

I'm currently in Spain, writing this while listening to the Mediterranean Sea crash against the shore. While I'm sitting here enjoying myself, a fully automated lead generation process is currently working for me, collecting email addresses of tax debtors that may be in need of my help to resolve their IRS collections matter. Those leads are automatically followed up with, nurtured, and moved forward in my sales funnel towards eventually becoming clients, either for myself or the professional colleague that I refer them out to.

This manual will guide you through the process of creating such an automated sales funnel for your own tax practice. We will delve into the technical mechanics of actually creating these systems, as well as exploring the minimum amount of search engine optimization, social media interaction, and other online marketing tactics that you can engage in to deliver qualified prospects to your sales funnel.

For some readers, this manual will become excessively technical. This is what you were promised when you were offered this manual, and it's what will be delivered to you. Some readers will find that the technical material is over their head, which is fine. The creation and management of all these processes is easily outsourced to any tech savvy high school or college student, or to a competent tech person you can find on Craigslist. Just as most of us advocate for all people having their "tax person", all business owners should have a "tech person" in their Rolodex.

Even if you don't create these systems yourself, you can provide this manual to your technology compatriot for them to handle it. I'd still suggest reading through the material, so that you understand what needs to be done and what it should look like in the end.

The approach used in this manual will be a simple one. It is presented from the standpoint of a licensed tax professional that is choosing to add a new service to their tax practice. In this case, it will be IRS collections representation, since that is what I know best and what the majority of my readers are interested in. We will walk through the creation of an entire new lead generation web site, and the marketing of that web site. You'll be able to see that site functional online by the time you receive this manual, and within these pages you'll be able to step through how it was built and marketed, complete with pretty pictures showing what I did and explanations for why.

For the practitioner adding new services to their practice, or just now coming around to understand the power and purpose of direct response marketing, a common question will arise:

Why do I need multiple web sites?

Firm Web Site vs Lead Generation Web Sites

Your primary firm web site is most likely a complicated beast.

Lead generation web sites, by definition, are extremely simple. They do not contain client portals, service menus, customer service contacts, etc. This is NOT your firm web site. While your firm web site should, of course, have it's own lead capture mechanism and associated funnel, it is a far more complex web site than we are talking about here.

Lead generation sites, by their very nature, are NOT full service. They do not, and should not, try to sell all your services to all visitors. Lead generation web sites generally have one sole purpose: **To collect contact information from visitors interested in ONE specific thing.**

When you collect this contact information, you now have a lead. This lead then needs to be nurtured over time through a systemized, heavily automated process. This automatic system helps the prospect to know more about you and your firm, what you can do for them, and how they can work with you. This process converts the *lead* into a *prospect*. Prospects are people that you have actually had a consultation or conversation with in regards to their needs. Never confuse a lead with a prospect.

In order for us to be on the same page in regards to lingo, let's go over some marketing terms that will be repeated throughout this manual.

Some Definitions

Sales funnel: A systematic set of interactions with an individual that gradually moves them closer and closer to making an actual purchase. The "funnel" analogy is used because you have a lot of people that enter in at the top, and over time a smaller number of people will progress to becoming prospects, and then even fewer will become clients. You will never convert 100% of leads into clients. All marketing systems of this nature are really *filtering mechanisms*, intended to help you identify ideal clients and only work with people that are truly qualified to be your client.

Lead magnets: Sometimes referred to by other names, such as "carrots" or "widgets", lead magnets are direct response mechanisms. In other words, the lead magnet is the item that the lead wants that prompts them to provide you their contact information. Lead magnets must have a reasonable perceived value to the person, otherwise they will not want it, and they will not provide you their contact information. These response vehicles usually take the form of a report, book, video, audio, or other form of *information*. It should be noted that one of the most frequently used lead magnets by professional service providers, the free consultation, actually has very low perceived value in the minds of consumer. Free consultations are an expectation in this day and age – they are nothing special and thus should NEVER be used as a lead magnet. It is acceptable to package the free consultation into something else, but "free consultation" itself is a nearly worthless lead generation mechanism today.

Autoresponder: An autoresponder is a piece of software that automatically sends out a pre-written message to a lead. Autoresponder systems are predominantly email-based, but such systems also exist for telephone, direct mail, fax, video, and even radio. Autoresponder systems, particularly email, are one of the most powerful sales funnel automation tools that exist on the planet, and failing to take advantage of this technology today is a major marketing sin.

Keywords: A set of words and phrases that humans enter into search engines in order to find something. For example, if you want to have a pizza delivered in Houston, you might search on Google for something like "fastest pizza delivery Houston". These phrases are important for you to know, so that you can include them in many places on your lead generation web site, as well as in other places off your site. The proper use of the right keyword phrases is one of the most critical components of actually getting people **to** your web site.

The Mechanics of Building Lead Generation Sites

Now that you understand why you need multiple web sites, and what the purpose of each is, let's delve into the mechanics. Yes, this is where we're going to get all technical on you.

Even if you choose to outsource this process to somebody else – even if you retain a full service suite such as that offered by Nate Hagerty's team at http://TaxFirmWebSites.com – I highly encourage you to digest the technical material in this section so that you have at least a basic understanding of what's going on behind the scenes.

When you create a *lead generation web site*, it has one purpose, as we discussed earlier. That sole purpose is to find you interested people that are interested in what you offer. **Nothing more, nothing less, and nothing else.**

If you're choosing to build these sites yourself, what you'll discover is that the first one might take you several days. Then, the second one takes you half that time. By your fifth such miniature web site, you'll be completing the entire basic setup process in a couple hours or less.

Here is the big picture process:

1. Conduct research into the keywords people actually use to search for what you offer.
2. Find a domain name that hopefully includes good keywords.
3. Obtain web hosting.
4. Tie the domain name to the web hosting.
5. Install WordPress.
6. Add a theme to WordPress.
7. Obtain an email autoresponder system.
8. Create follow up emails
9. Create signup form.
10. Place signup form into WordPress site.
11. Set up blog post broadcaster.
12. Create an editorial schedule.
13. Upload report and add link to email.

Step 1: Keyword research

There are numerous keyword research tools available online, both free and paid. However, I still think it's best to go straight to the source, and tap into data directly from the largest search engine on the planet.

To do this, you'll need a Google Adwords account (even if you don't plan to buy ads on Google). To register for a Google Adwords account, go here:

http://adwords.google.com

and click the "Get Started Now" button. You'll then walk through an account setup process. Registering for an Adwords account is free. If you do want to run ads, do a Google search for "free adwords credit" and you'll find promotion codes for up to $100 worth of free Adwords credits that you can use.

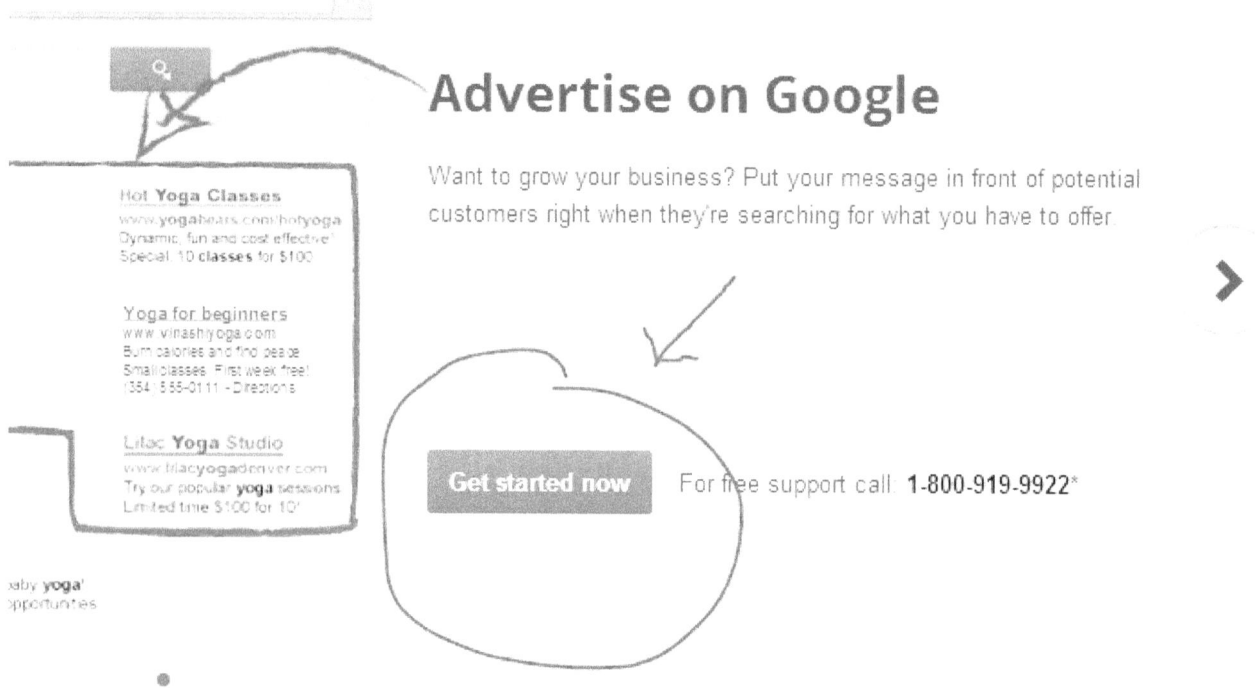

Once you have your Adwords account set up, you then have to access the Keyword Planner, which is what we're really after here. Once your Adwords account has loaded, you'll see a menu across the top. Select the "Tools" menu, and from the dropdown, select "Keyword Planner".

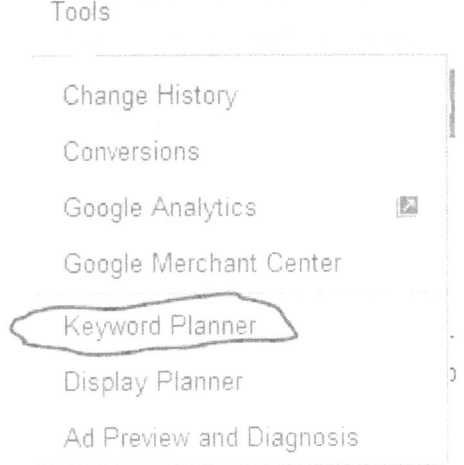

Once the Keyword Planner screen loads, select "Search for new keyword and ad group ideas."

Keyword Planner
Plan your next search campaign

What would you like to do?

- Search for new keyword and ad group ideas

- Get search volume for a list of keywords or group them into ad groups

- Get traffic estimates for a list of keywords

- Multiply keyword lists to get new keyword ideas

In the input boxes, I usually only enter a few keywords in order to see what Google suggests. It's also a good idea to limit your search to the United States. If you're not sure what to enter, enter the *name of your service*. In other words, if you're doing this for your tax planning services, then enter "tax planning". If you're doing this for your financial planning services, then enter "financial planning".

If you are only looking to create a site to collect leads in your local area, add common terms for your local area. For example, enter "tax planning Houston" if that is your service and market area.

TaxMarketingHQ.com

If you have been looking at established web sites, you can enter the URL of that web site and Google will automatically extract keyword suggestions from it. That's another way to get started. For example, you could enter the URL of the site I'm creating as the example for this manual (whatever it ends up being, we haven't selected it yet as I'm writing this sequentially).

So here's what this might look like to start:

▼ Search for new keyword and ad group ideas

Enter one or more of the following:

Your product or service

```
1040 tax liabilities
irs tax attorneys
```

Your landing page

www.example.com/page

Your product category

Enter or select a product category

Targeting ?
United States
English
Google
Negative keywords

Customize your search ?

Keyword filters

Keyword options
Show broadly related ideas
Hide keywords in my account
Hide keywords in my plan

Include/Exclude

Get ideas

The actual keywords I entered to start with were:

tax resolution
irs tax debt help
payroll tax debts
1040 tax liabilities
irs tax attorneys

I started with these keywords because they identify the actual service I'm selling, and are keywords that I think people might actually use to search for the service. It's important to note

TaxMarketingHQ.com

that what YOU would search for as a tax professional is most likely different from what an actual consumer would search for. We have a professional knowledge bias about terminology and jargon that consumers don't have. For example, most consumers aren't even aware of that term "tax resolution". That's an industry term. Thus, I tried to think like a consumer, and what they might search for. Google's Keyword Planner will, of course, fill in the blanks and provide better ideas, but it's a place to start.

Here are the results from this particular search on the day that I was writing this:

Ad group (by relevance)	Keywords	Avg. monthly searches	Competition	Suggested bid	Ad impr. share	Add to plan
Irs Help (23)	help with irs tax debt, ir...	4,580	High	$11.36	0%	
Tax Debt (27)	payroll tax debt relief, b...	1,130	High	$20.55	0%	
Irs Back (21)	irs back tax help, irs ba...	630	High	$23.85	0%	
Tax Bracket (7)	irs tax brackets, tax bra...	129,190	Low	$1.75	0%	
Irs Form (10)	irs tax forms, irs tax for...	270,330	Medium	$1.61	0%	
Tax Resolution (33)	tax debt resolution, tax ...	4,260	High	$29.34	0%	
Tax Forms (7)	tax forms, federal tax fo...	46,910	High	$2.69	0%	

You'll notice that there are two tabs in the search results: Ad group ideas, and keyword ideas. The ad group ideas are Google's suggestions for clusters of keywords to use for the same ad that you would run on their site. If you hover your mouse over the "keywords" column, you'll see a small popup that shows the actual keywords in that keyword group.

Notice that Google groups keywords in an organized fashion. Google knows what to group together, because they know what people are searching for, and ultimately what they click on. They won't share that raw data with us, unfortunately, but these summaries are pretty nice.

In these results, I'm most interested in the "irs help", "tax debt", and "tax resolution" ad group suggestions. You can see the average number of monthly searches for each group, and the advertising competition for each group, also. Note that the highest monthly search group is not necessarily our best option. You'll see that between the three groups of interest, "irs help" and "tax resolution" have the highest search volumes, and they both have high competition. But, the suggested ad bid for "irs help" is significantly lower.

The suggested bid is the amount that Google suggests you should pay PER CLICK in order to advertise on Adwords with that ad group, in order to have a successful campaign. These high prices are a good reason NOT to advertise on Google, but we'll get into that later.

If you click over to the keywords tab, you'll see a breakdown of these same factors on an individual keyword basis. That list can be particularly useful, and you can even download it as a spreadsheet in order to sift and sort in Excel. We'll get to that in a moment.

For now, I want to make note of the keywords in each ad group. I've taken screen shots of the pop ups that appear if you hover over each ad group:

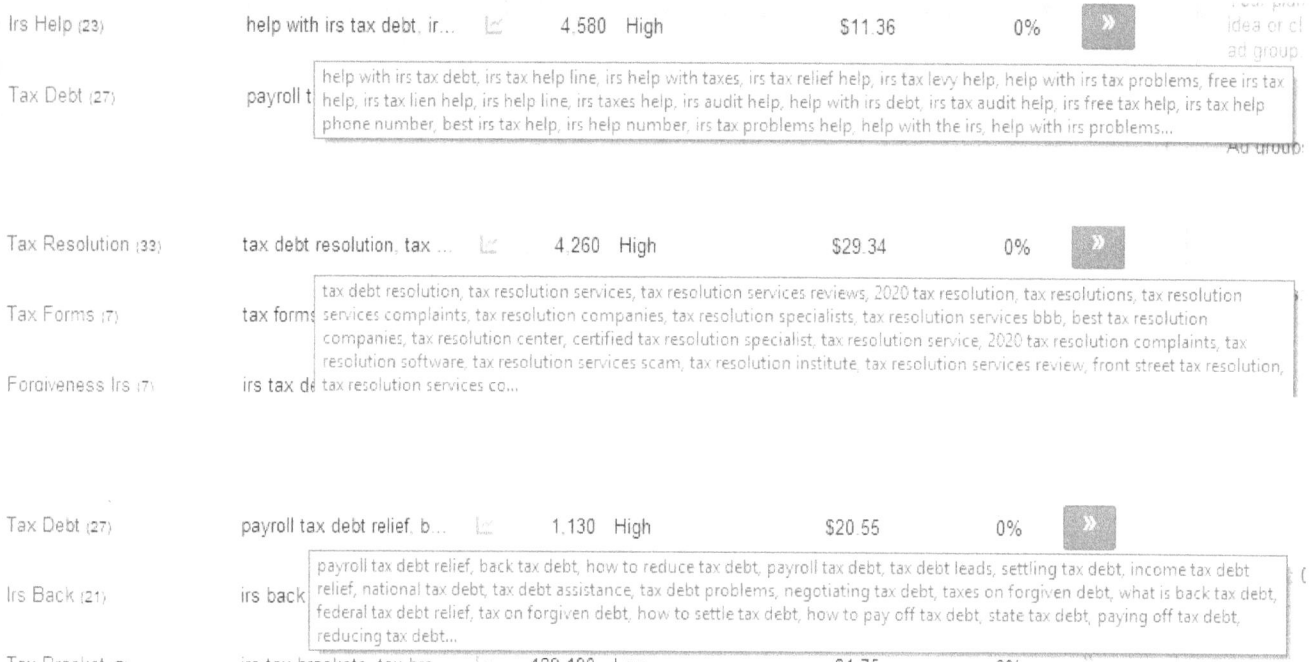

You'll notice that the exact keywords in each of these ad group ideas falls into three general categories. The first group, "irs help", is all about people looking for help with specific types of IRS problems. The second group, "tax resolution", contains a lot of keywords related to consumer searches for reviews and complaints of specific tax resolution firms. The third group, "tax debt", contains a lot of keywords that appear to be research oriented.

Please pay attention to this, particularly in relation to our overall objective. We're trying to build a lead generation site – we're looking for people that are ready to take action. In other words, we want **buyer-based keywords**, not research-based keywords. We want to focus on searchers that are looking for service providers, rather than searchers that are simply looking for information.

With that in mind, I'm going to throw out the "tax debt" group from consideration. But what about the second group?

There are countless successful lead generation web sites, in numerous industries, that are **review sites**, and this is a perfectly valid approach to this project. In fact, there is a very successful lead generation blog in the tax resolution space for a firm in Seattle, and it's nothing but a massive review site, listing nearly every national tax resolution firm in existence. Since only one other person is really doing this right now, there is an opportunity to create something competitive to it within the tax resolution space. Somebody reading this manual would be well served by taking this approach (seriously, this is a million-dollar idea for the right person reading this right now).

This approach is not the one I'm going to take for this example, however. As a "classically trained" direct response marketer, I prefer taking an educational approach to all my marketing. In other words, I prefer educating my customers through informative materials, and I'll be sticking with that approach for this example. However, as stated, **somebody reading this manual should build a review site.**

So, I've settled on ad group number one. In case it's difficult to read the small type, here are some of the keywords listed in that ad group. This is not the entire keyword list, just the ones more relevant to tax resolution:

help with irs tax debt
irs tax relief help
irs tax levy help
help with irs tax problems
irs tax lien help
irs audit help
help with irs debt
irs tax audit help
best irs tax help
irs tax problems help
help with irs problems

Notice that most of these keywords are variations of the same thing. There are common words contained across most of them: help, tax, irs. I'm going to throw out the suggestions containing the word "audit", since I focus on collections representation, not audit representation.

I'm then going to take the remaining keywords from this ad group, and do a new search in Keyword Planner with them.

▼ Search for new keyword and ad group ideas

Enter one or more of the following:
Your product or service

```
help with irs tax debt
irs tax relief help
```

Your landing page

www.example.com/page

Your product category

Enter or select a product category

Targeting ?
United States

Customize your search ?
Keyword filters

With this new keyword search, I'm now going to click over to the "Keyword Ideas" tab:

Ad group ideas	Keyword ideas				Download
Search terms		Avg. monthly searches ?	Competition ?	Suggested bid ?	Ad impr. share ?
help with irs debt		140	High	$29.73	0%
help with irs problems		70	High	$34.03	0%
help with irs tax problems		50	High	$47.13	0%
help with irs tax debt		50	High	$34.98	0%
irs tax relief help		40	High	$30.41	0%
irs tax levy help		40	High	$43.22	0%
irs tax lien help		30	High	$61.44	0%
irs tax problems help		20	High	$29.38	0%

Notice that the Suggested Bid for a lot of these keywords is incredibly high. What this means is that, despite the low monthly search volume, advertisers are competing extremely aggressively within the Adwords advertising platform to have their ads show up first when

Google users do a search for these phrases. Those prices are per click, which is why I do not generally suggest advertising on Adwords. There are simply more affordable ways to go about this.

Scrolling through the results list, you'll see data for the keywords you entered, but below that are additional suggestions. Many of the suggestions will have nothing to do with what we're actually looking for, so we need to be careful about which ones we look at.

Looking through these results, it's becoming clear that I want a domain name that includes some combination of the following words: irs, help, tax, problem, debt. There are some additional words, such as "back" or "lien" that I could also add if necessary to find a good domain. With all this information, I'm now ready to look for a domain name.

Step 2: Find a domain name.

One of the problems with finding a good domain name these days is that most of the best ones are taken. It can be a challenge to find a good name, especially a .com name, which is still the gold standard, despite all the new TLDs (Top Level Domains) that are coming available these days. TLDS are the domain endings, like com, net, info, biz, us, co, etc. If at all possible, you want a .com name.

Using my list of words from the Google Keyword planner, I'm going to try finding a good domain name. Please note that I'm unlikely to find a domain name that's not taken for a specific keyword. For example, irstaxhelp.com (and .org, .net., etc) is taken. But my goal is to find something close that contains the words in a logical phrase.

Why am I concerned about this? **Having a keyword phrase as your domain name helps with your position in search results.** This is becoming less and less of a factor in the SEO process, according to Google, but real world results indicate that it's still a fairly relevant factor.

Here are my words from the Keyword Planner:

IRS
Help
Tax
Problem
Debt
Back
Lien

I started by going to what is my current favorite domain registration provider. I'm in the process of migrating ALL of my domain names (I have almost a hundred of them…). Their prices are slightly higher than GoDaddy, but all domains come with private registration. This keeps your email address, mailing address, and phone number private in the public domain name databases, which cuts down on spam and other annoyances. They also don't have the annoying 60 day lock policy that GoDaddy has, which has cost me money in the past (a story for another time).

Since my favorite domain name registrar might change in the future, I'm creating a referential link that will always forward to whatever I'm currently using. I'll update this in the future if my preferences ever change:

http://TaxMarketingHQ.com/domains

I started by searching for exact phrases from the keyword planner.

TaxMarketingHQ.com

HelpWithIRSDebt.com — Make Offer / Whois

HelpWithIRSDebt.net — Make Offer / Whois

The first Keyword Planner idea is taken.

Next....

irstaxproblemhelp.com — Make Offer / Whois

irstaxproblemhelp.net — Make Offer / Whois

irstaxproblemhelp.org — Make Offer / Whois

irstaxproblemhelp.us — Make Offer / Whois

Also taken… This can get frustrating, so I'll save you the time and get straight to the one that worked:

irsbacktaxproblemhelp.com	$10.69/year
irsbacktaxproblemhelp.net	$11.98/year
irsbacktaxproblemhelp.org	$11.48/year
irsbacktaxproblemhelp.us	$7.99/year
irsbacktaxproblemhelp.info	$10.47/year

Success!

IRSBackTaxProblemHelp.com was available, so I snapped it up.

Now that I have a domain name, I now need a place to put it, which leads us to Step 3…

Step 3: Web hosting

Web hosting refers to the physical computer on which your web site sits. Most people don't think much about this, especially if your primary firm web site is operated by a large company that specializes in offering turnkey sites. If you operate your own site, then you may be familiar with this idea already.

But if you're not, here's what web hosting is: You rent physical hard drive space, on a real computer (called a server), that sits in a massive, air conditioned room full of such servers, all connected directly to massive, high speed fiber optic Internet connections (called "backbone" connections).

These server farms exist in expensive data centers at key fiber optic crossroad points (hubs). Typical locations include Houston, Chicago, New York, London, Singapore, etc. Companies that own these data centers lease out space to smaller companies that actually install the servers and sell the hosting.

If you already have a hosting account that allows you to add additional domain names and web sites to, then great. I personally keep two very separate hosting accounts, at two different companies. One account is called a VPS (Virtual Private Server), which I use for my primary web sites that require greater resources and absolutely must stay up at all times (taxmarketinghq.com sits on the VPS, for example). This service costs me $67 per month.

All of my smaller sites, particularly lead generation sites, sit on a much cheaper shared hosting account that I only pay about $10 per month for. This hosting service allows me to add an unlimited number of additional domains and web sites. I use the Business plan at the following hosting provider, although their "Baby" plan is just as good for most folks, and only runs about $7 per month:

http://TaxMarketingHQ.com/hosting

If I ever change my recommendation, the above link will automatically route to that new company. But I've been with this outfit for close to a decade, so doubt I'll change anytime soon.

Here's how to add a domain name to a CPanel-based web hosting account. CPanel is an administration interface for web hosting companies, and is the most popular such interface. This web interface allows you to perform complex operations inside the actual UNIX operating system that the web hosting runs on, without having to know all the command line commands for doing it.

Assuming your web hosting account, like mine, allows you to add additional add on domains, here is what you do. After logging into your CPanel interface, click the "Addon Domains" button:

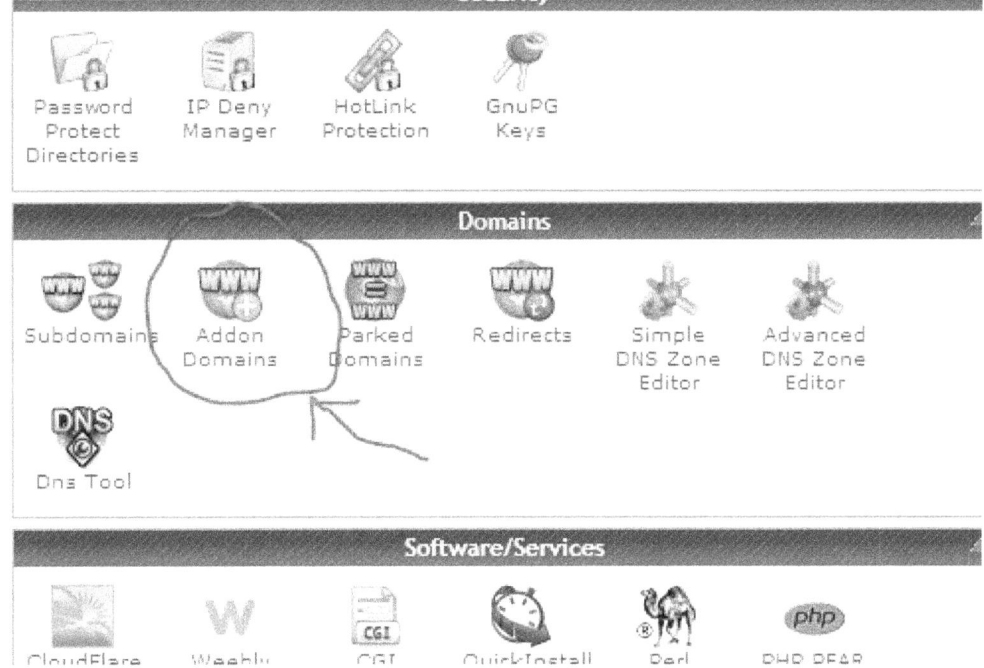

On the next page, you'll presented with the following screen in CPanel:

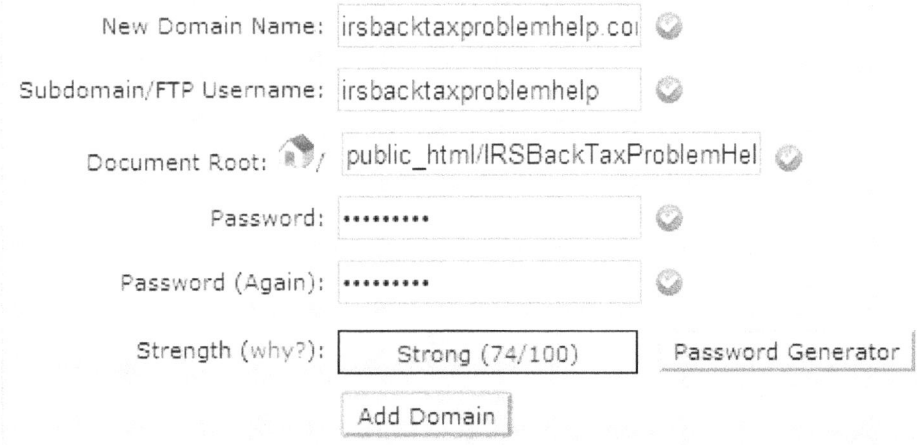

The new domain name goes into the appropriate field. Notice that it does not contain the "http" or the "www", it's just the raw domain name. The system will automatically fill in your username, document, and then you enter a secure password, twice, then click "Add Domain".

Voila! It's done. Next, we need to update the Internet DNS to point your domain name to this hosting account.

Step 4: Tie domain name to web hosting (Update DNS)

DNS stands for Domain Name Service. The entire Internet actually runs on a numerical addressing system, called IP addresses. These numbers are how all Internet traffic, including web, FTP, email, etc., all knows where to go. Remember those servers we discussed in the last step? Each of those servers has a number, which might look something like this: 214.34.4.1. This address serves the same purpose as your home street address, and tells the world where to find you.

Since the Internet works on this numerical system, which isn't very useful to us humans, we use the DNS system to translate domain names, which you and I can read, into these numerical addresses. In order to tell the Internet which numerical address your domain name should point to, we need to update the DNS records at the place where you registered your domain name.

Your web hosting provider will provide you one or more name servers to use. These name servers need to be entered into your domain registrar. Here is how I do this with my domain provider:

On the domain information screen, click the "Transfer DNS to Webhost". On many other registrars, including GoDaddy, this will just say "Update DNS Servers" or something to that effect.

My web hosting provider has sent me an email containing all my account info (*NEVER* delete that email, you'll need it forever). Name servers are usually in the format of "nsXXX.something.com", where XXX is a number. I'm simply going to copy and paste the name servers from that email into the form at my domain registrar:

Modify Domain: irsbacktaxproblemhelp.com

ENTER YOUR CUSTOM DOMAIN NAME SERVER INFORMATION

You are currently using our domain name servers (DNS) for your domain.

You can change it and start using your own name servers or name servers of someo else like your webhost. This step is sometimes known as 'transferring the domain' by some webhosts. Please note that using custom nameservers will disable some of our free features like e-mail forwarding, url forwarding etc., as these functionalities depend on our nameservers.

Please enter DNS name only (ex: ns1.mydomain.com). Please don't enter IP addresses. You can enter up to five name servers. It is advisable to enter atleast two nameservers for a domain. Please note that it will take up to 24 hours for the changes to take effect.
Please note that if you are setting up DNS servers for .eu or .ca domains, use the IPAddress--dns.name format (ex: 12.12.32.22--ns1.domain.com)

○ Use Namecheap Hosting DNS Servers
◉ Specify Custom DNS Servers (Your own DNS Servers)

1. ns▮▮▮▮▮▮.com
2. ns▮▮▮▮▮▮.com
3.
4.
5.

Add More Nameservers

Save Changes

After pasting both in, I'm going to hit "Save Changes". And that's it.

Do note that it usually takes a couple hours for DNS changes to be updated across the Internet, and it can take up to 48 hours (although this is rare these days). Your domain registrar has to send these changes to DNS root servers, which are centralized addressing databases all over the world. After this updating takes place, your new web site will be accessible from everywhere.

Now, we need to actually put something up for the world to see. This becomes the fun part.

Step 5: Install WordPress.

With a blank web hosting account, the web server has nothing to show the world. Here's the error message you're likely to see if you try to access your new domain name from your web browser:

Forbidden

You don't have permission to access / on this server.

Additionally, a 500 Internal Server Error error was encountered while trying to use an ErrorDocument to handle the request.

Apache Server at irsbacktaxproblemhelp.com Port 80

The reason that this error message shows up is because there is nothing sitting on our web hosting account for the web server to push out to the world when somebody visits. To correct this, let's installed WordPress.

Wordpress is the most popular blogging platform in the world, and one of the most flexible and user friendly web management systems available. It is estimated that about 19% of all web sites on the Internet are running WordPress.

Within CPanel, it becomes pretty easy to install WordPress via the Fantastico software installer.

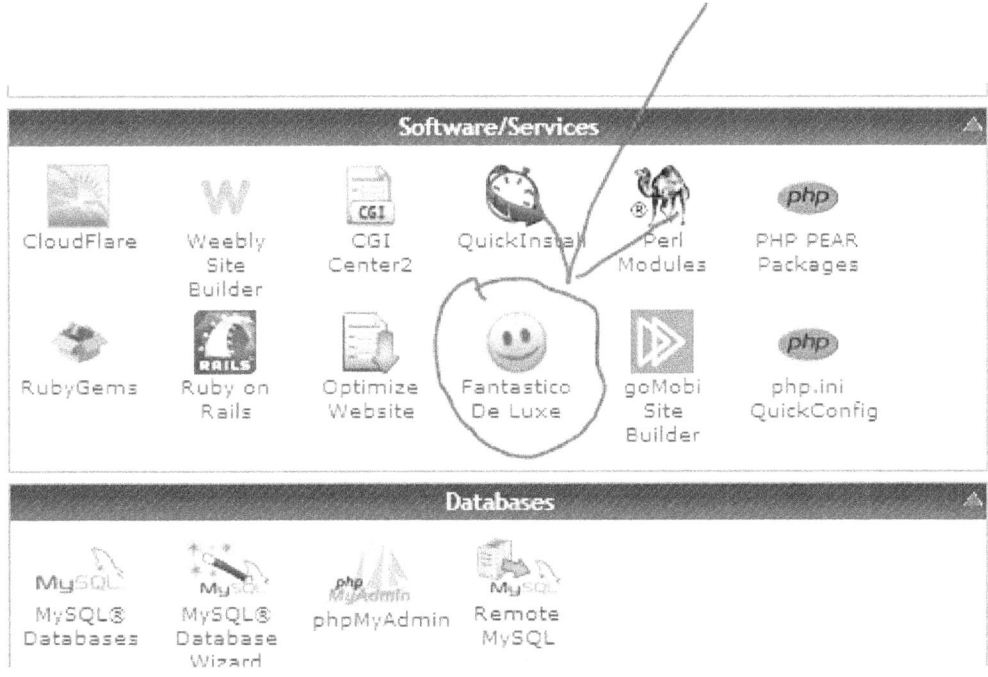

Once inside Fantastico, click the WordPress link:

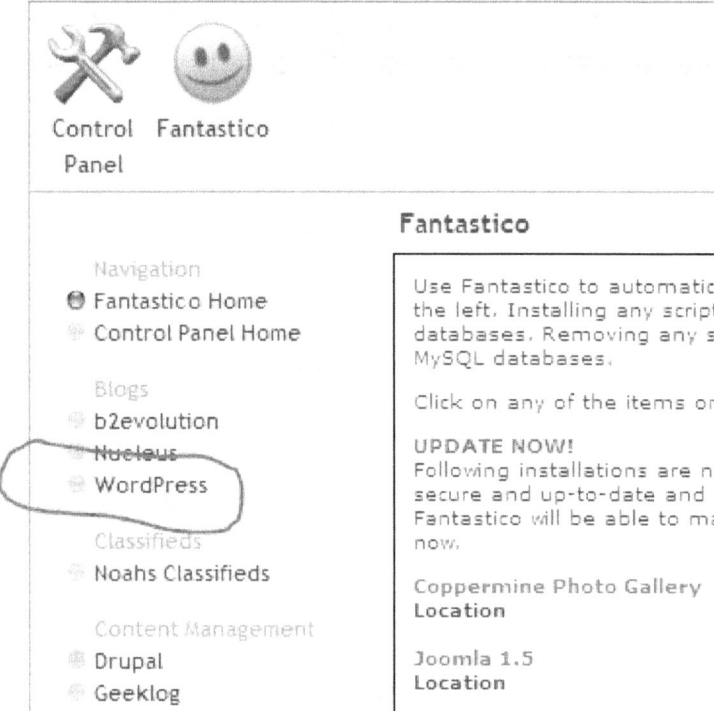

Then click the link for a "New Installation" of WordPress:

This will take you to an installation options page. You'll need to enter the domain name for your site, an admin username, an email address, site description, and a few other items. Note that you should leave the "install directory" blank, since we want to use WordPress to run our entire site, not just a specifc sub-directory.

After filling in these options, click "Install WordPress". This will take you to an installation confirmation screen. On this screen, be sure to press "Finish Installation" in order to actually have WordPress install the necessary software files.

After WordPress finishes installing, you'll be presented with a page that gives you the option to email the installation details to an email address. It is highly advised to send this email to yourself, and to keep it in a safe place for future reference should you ever need it again.

Step 6: Add a theme to WordPress.

When you first install Wordpress, it comes with a default look, feel, and layout, called the *theme*. The current default WordPress theme, in my personal opinion, is ugly. The 2013 default theme was even worse, however. I'm a big fan of the 2011 and 2012 default themes, however.

In addition, there are literally tens of thousands of user-developed themes available for you to download. Many paid themes, called *premium themes*, provide various special features. However, there are so many good free themes to choose from that you really don't need to buy a premium theme if you don't want to.

In general, I tend to be a big fan of the premium themes put out by WooThemes.com. All of my primary web sites run WooThemes, and I'm gradually transitioning all my sites to their Canvas theme framework.

For lead generation sites in particular, such as what we're building here, I much prefer layouts that are incredibly *clean*. In this day and age of complex web site layouts, I still find that clean and simple are best. Clean sites load faster, and have fewer distractions, allowing you to direct your visitors more appropriately down the path you want them to take.

Here is the default WordPress 2014 theme as it looks when you first install WordPress:

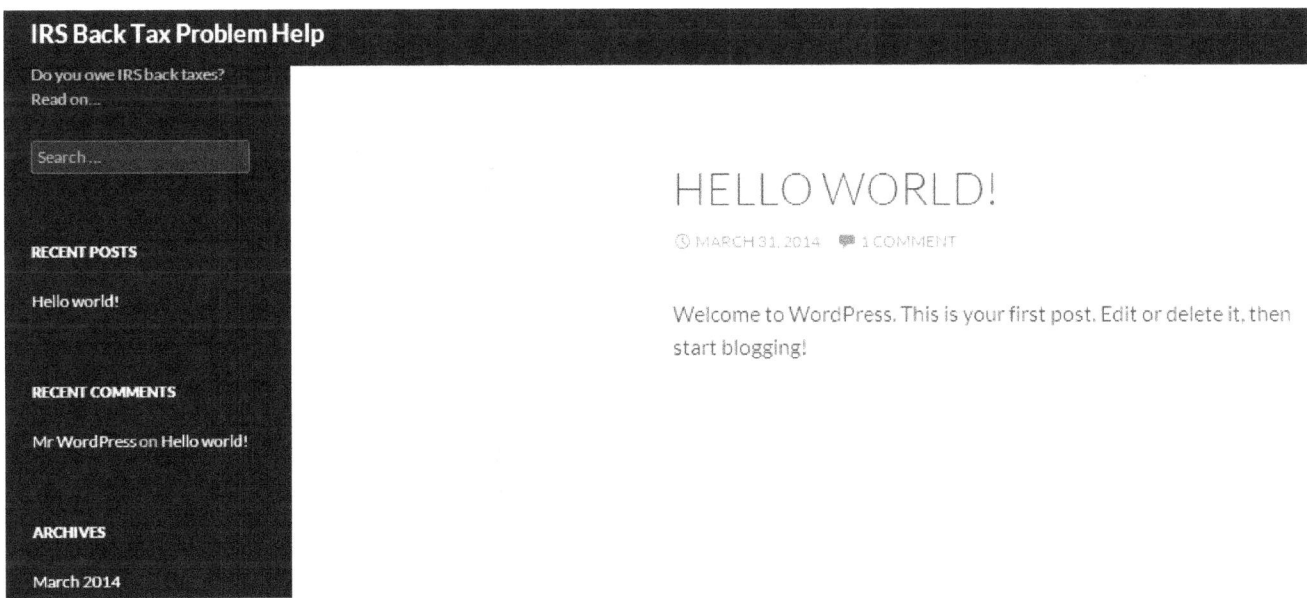

I'm going to change this from the 2014 theme to the 2012 theme:

TaxMarketingHQ.com

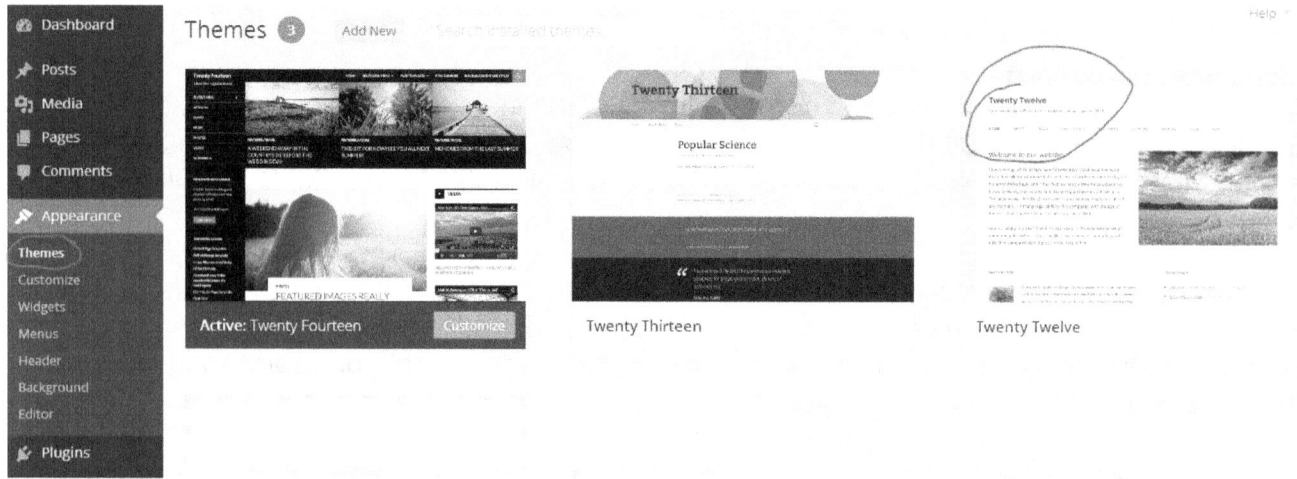

To change the theme, simply click "Appearance", then "Themes", then select the theme that you want.

Side note: One of my favorite non-default themes is a free theme called Tycho. You can install this, or any other free theme from the Wordpress theme directory, by clicking the "Add New" button at the top of the theme page, and searching for a theme.

We're now going to customize the 2012 theme by clicking on the customize button:

I changed the header title color to blue, and made sure that the front page was set to show the latest posts. Then, click "Save and Publish":

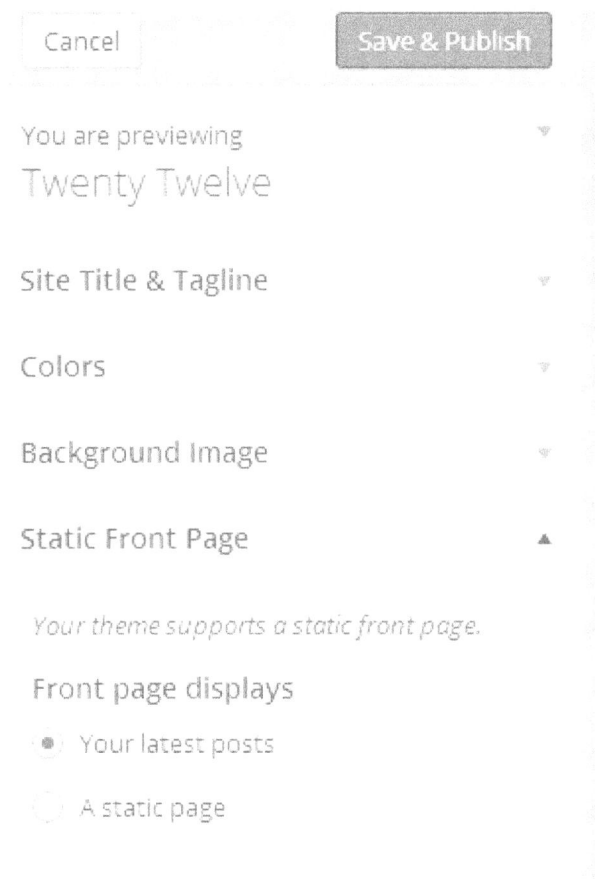

I'm now going to do a few other things to clean up the look of the site. Under "Appearance" on the left side of the WordPress admin menu, I'm now going to click the "Widgets" link. Widgets are the extra stuff that appears on the right side of the site layout. Eventually, we're going to add an offer with an opt-in form to the very top position, where the search box sits now. But we're also going to delete a few unnecessary things.

Widgets

Available Widgets

To activate a widget drag it to a sidebar or click on it. To deactivate a widget and delete its settings, drag it back.

Archives	Calendar
A monthly archive of your site's Posts.	A calendar of your site's Posts.

Categories	Custom Menu
A list or dropdown of categories.	Add a custom menu to your sidebar.

Meta	Pages
Login, RSS, & WordPress.org links.	A list of your site's Pages.

Recent Comments	Recent Posts
Your site's most recent comments.	Your site's most recent Posts.

RSS	Search

Main Sidebar

Appears on posts and pages except the optional Front Page template, which has its own widgets

Search

Title:

Delete | Close

[Save]

Recent Posts

Recent Comments

Archives

Categories

Meta

Click the little triangle on each sidebar widget to expand it, then click the "Delete" link for each item to be deleted. I deleted the search, recent comments, archives, and meta widgets.

After that, here is what the page now looks like:

IRS Back Tax Problem Help

Do you owe IRS back taxes? Read on...

HOME   SAMPLE PAGE

Hello world!

1 Reply

Welcome to WordPress. This is your first post. Edit or delete it, then start blogging!

This entry was posted in Uncategorized on March 31, 2014. Edit

RECENT POSTS

Hello world!

CATEGORIES

Uncategorized

Note that some of the default installation stuff still doesn't fit very well for us. The only existing category is called "Uncategorized", and there is one post called "Hello World!" and a sample page called exactly that. We need to change these items. Here's what to click to enter the editor for each of these items:

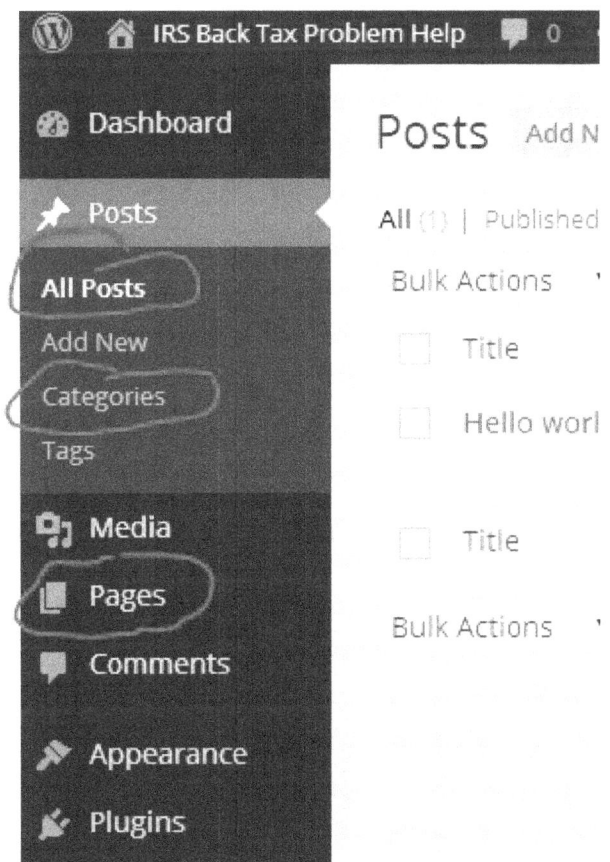

First, I'm going to edit the default category. I'm going to label it as another keyword phrase from our earlier keyword research. For now, I'm going to simply change it to "Tax Resolution". On the Categories admin page, place the cursor underneath "uncategorized", and select "edit".

Edit Category

Name Tax Resolution
The name is how it appears on your site.

Slug tax-resolution
The "slug" is the URL-friendly version of the name. It is usually all lowerca

Parent None ▼
Categories, unlike tags, can have a hierarchy. You might have a Jazz categ Totally optional.

Description Tax resolution strategies for resolving IRS back tax problems.

The description is not prominent by default; however, some themes may show it.

[Update]

Note that I also included a category description that includes a keyword-rich phrase. This is a tiny but worthwhile search engine optimization thing.

I'll then click "Update" to save the changes, and proceed to edit the default "Hello World" post.

I'm going to change the post title, the body of the post, and also change the permalink structure. This is pretty important from an SEO standpoint. Notice that the default permalink structure is domain.com/?p=1. That doesn't do us much good. We want it to be something more like domain.com/post-title, so we're going to change it something more user friendly and better for SEO purposes. When I click the "Change Permalinks" button it takes me to this page:

I'm going to select "Post name" and then save the changes.

I then went back to the post editor and changed the post title and added a few paragraphs of content. This was just a really quick, off the cuff little post about the OIC program.

I'm next going to delete the one default comment, by clicking on the "Comments" button on the left side of the admin bar, then click on the "Trash" link that shows up when you hover your mouse over the comment text.

Next, let's create one of the most important pages on any web site by changing the "Sample Page" to an "About" page. To do this, click "Pages" in the left side admin bar, then underneath "Sample Page" select "Edit".

One of the mistakes that I see almost every tax professional make on their web is that their "About" page is full of tripe. Basically, most "About" pages are just customer service platitudes and hyperbole. Most tax professionals don't even put their NAME on their about page – as if they're trying to hide behind their web page.

This is a tremendous mistake. Never forget that people do business with people, not companies. People also do business with people that they *know, like,* and *trust.* Having a vague "About" page that says nothing about YOU does not build trust. Since your "About" page will be visited by at least 1/3 of all people that come to your site according to studies published by the Google Analytics team, it literally is the most important page on your blog.

While far from perfect, I'd invite you to take a look at my "About" page on my tax practice web site:

http://taxhelphq.com/about/

Note the difference between that and many other tax firm web site "About" pages.

For purposes of this sample site, I'll create a quick intro, and leave the rest blank to be filled in with photos and bios later:

Notice the "Edit" button that I've circled. Since this is a default sample page that we're editing, you'll want to change the permalink by clicking that edit button and changing the underlined text to "about". Change the text, click "OK", then click the "Update" button for the whole page to save the change.

Here's what our layout looks like now:

> *TaxMarketingHQ.com*
>
> # IRS Back Tax Problem Help
> Do you owe IRS back taxes? Read on...
>
> HOME   ABOUT
>
> ### The Truth About IRS Reduced Settlements
>
> Leave a reply
>
> As you investigate your options for addressing your IRS back tax problem, you will begin to hear a lot about settling your tax debt for "pennies on the dollar". In fact, many of the unlicensed sales reps you are likely to speak with at many big tax resolution companies will bend over backwards to guarantee you that you can settle for "pennies on the dollar".
>
> **Unfortunately, these claims simply are not true.**
>
> Be wary of anybody trying to sell you on an IRS reduced settlement program, called an Offer in Compromise. The reality of the tax code is that in order to qualify for this program, you
>
> RECENT POSTS
>
> The Truth About I
>
> CATEGORIES
>
> Tax Resolution

Notice that it's not flashy. It's not fancy. There are no graphics. It loads fast. Simple, simple, simple. **Do not overthink your lead page design.**

There are definitely additional things you can do to this site, such as social media sharing plugins, SEO plugins, etc. But DO NOT be concerned about those things until you actually have the site created, and have completed a bunch of online marketing steps to actually get eyeballs on the page. Until you have eyeballs, nothing else is necessary for this site, except an **offer** and **content**, which you'll discuss in the next few steps.

Step 7: Obtain an email autoresponder system.

Since we're assembling a fully automated, online lead generation funnel, we're going to need an automated email system, called an *autoresponder*.

There are a number of popular, reliable email systems out there that would work just fine for our purposes. Companies such as Aweber, MailChimp, ConstantContact, iContact, SendPepper, and InfusionSoft all provide good systems, with varying features and pricing.

My current recommendation for an email autoresponder provider will always be available from this link:

http://TaxMarketingHQ.com/email

As of the time of this writing, I use Aweber. They were an early pioneer in the reliable email platform game, and I've been using them off and on for almost ten years. The demo for this book will be based on their system.

To get started, let's first register for an account:

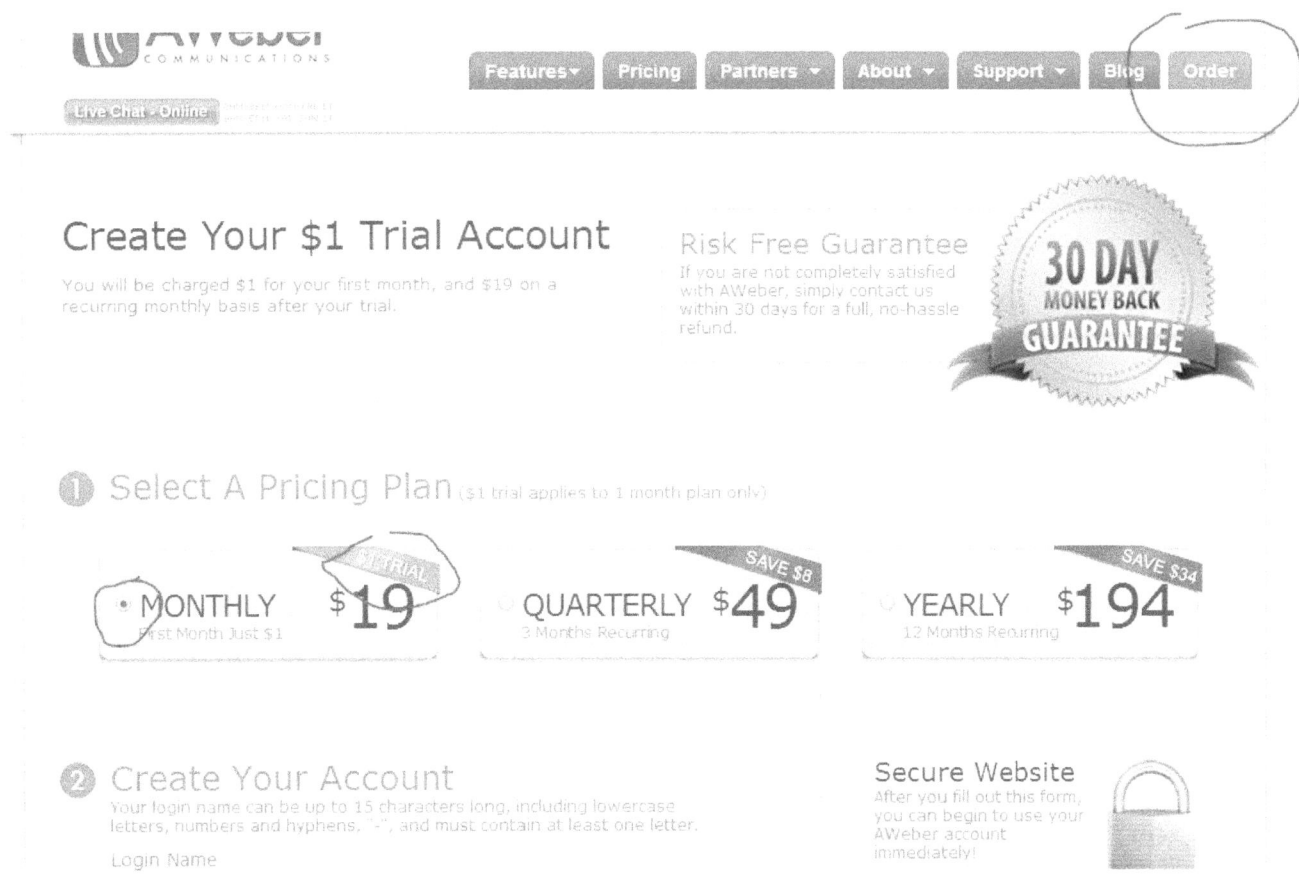

Right now, Aweber has a special promotion going whereby you get the first month for a dollar. This promo has actually been going on for as long as I remember, but they could obviously change it at any time.

Once you've signed up for an account, we need to create a new list. Aweber lets you create an unlimited number of separate lists, which comes in handy for segregating your lead streams as your marketing gets more sophisticated.

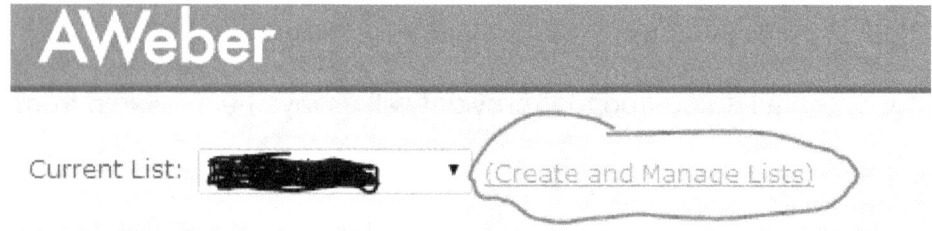

To create a new list in Aweber, click the "Create and Manage Lists" link at the top of the page in the account admin area after logging in. This will take you to the "Manage Your Lists" page, and then you can click "Create A List".

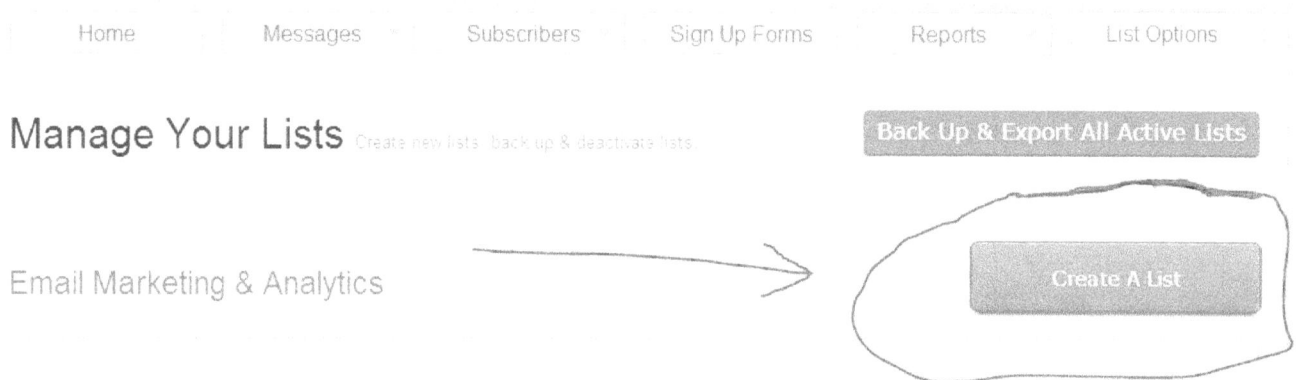

You'll then be taken to the list creation wizard. Aweber provides a video that explains the list creation process. If this is your first time using the system, I'd highly suggest taking the time to watch their demo video.

Also note that the wizard provides guidance through the list creation process. Even after using the system for years, I still keep the wizard running, and just step through the process as they say to. It's faster than navigating around their system independently using the normal navigation links.

On the basic information screen, fill in the name you want to give your list, your address, and other info as indicated. The "from" name and address is the name and address that will emails will appear to come from. It's best to make this your real name and a real email address that can be replied to, preferably using the domain name we're running the site on.

TaxMarketingHQ.com

After saving these basic settings, we next need to configure the confirmation message. All Aweber lists must use what is called "double opt-in", meaning that all requests for information by a user must be confirmed in order to prevent spam abuse.

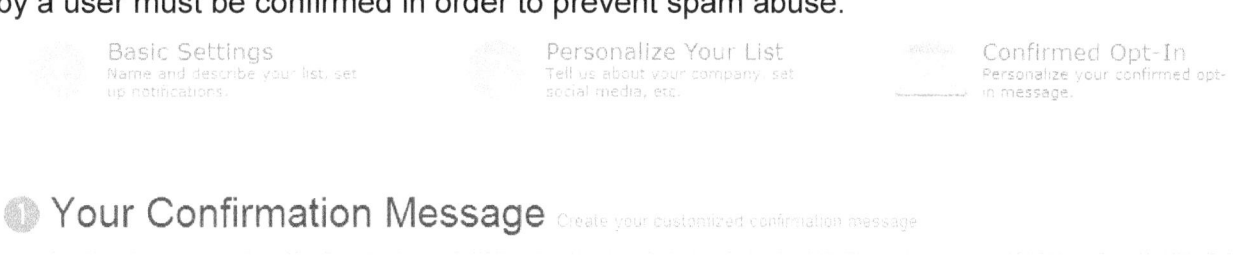

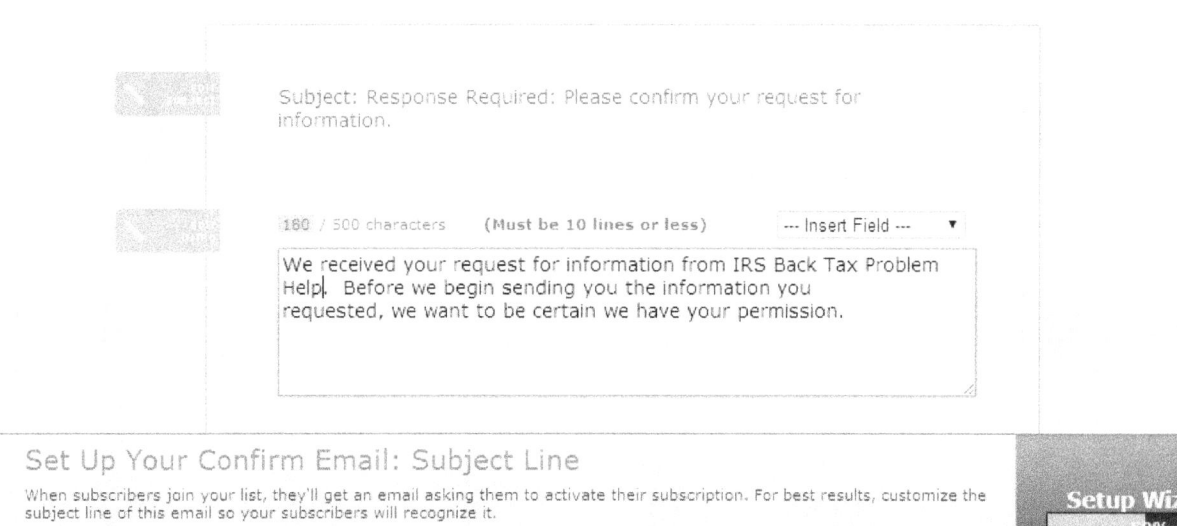

© 2014 Jassen Bowman & TaxMarketingHQ.com   Page 43

Notice that you can edit the subject and body of the confirmation message, and also add a closing.

When somebody successfully confirms their opt-in to receive information, you need to send them to another web page. In almost all situations, this is going to be a page where they can download the free report we are offering. This page doesn't exist yet, but we will create it later. As you can see here, it will be the "Welcome" page.

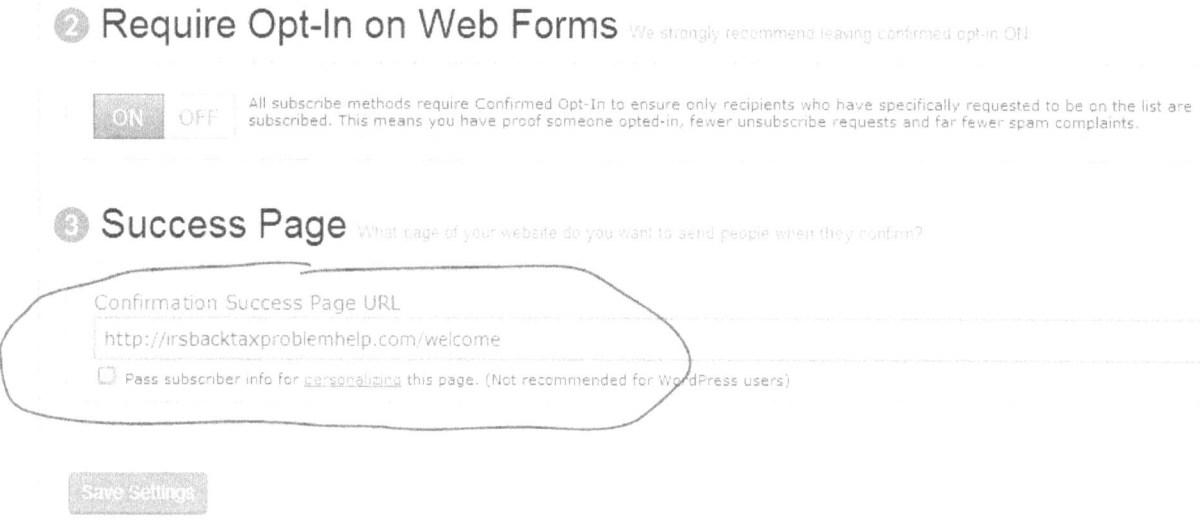

Step 8: Create follow up emails.

The next step in our process is to create our first follow up message. After subscribers confirm their opt-in, the next step is to send them the first email. Using the list creation wizard, we just click the "Do This Step" to be taken to that section of the admin interface.

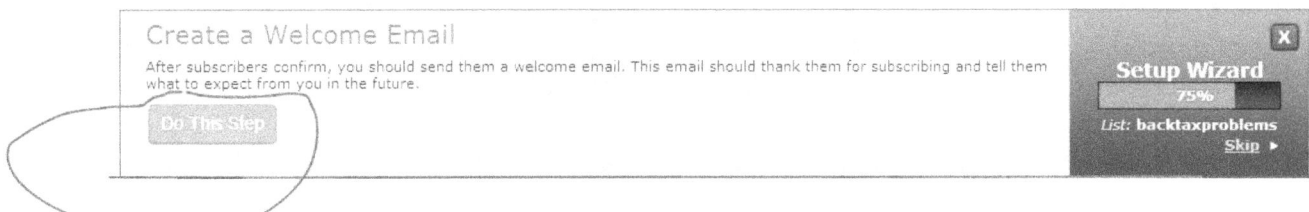

On the follow up message editor, you'll need to enter an email subject line, and text in the body of the email. Notice here that we are including a link back to our special report, even though after confirmation our new lead was directed to a "Welcome" page that also includes the link. We'll upload the actual report to WordPress later on, and come back and fill in the blank section where this link should be.

You'll notice that there is nothing fancy, special, or tricky about this message. I wrote this entirely off the cuff, with no preplanning or forethought. When most practitioners start this process, they get bogged down in the small things, such as trying to create the perfect email. I've worked with tax professionals that have not been able to get over this one simple thing, and they allow it to bog them down for *months*.

The concept of "don't overthink it" definitely applies to your follow up emails. The key is to just write them. Basically, write the exact same email that you would send to a close friend if they asked you for advice on this particular problem. Friendly and conversational is always good. The important part is to just get something created and in the system. You can (and should) go back and improve on the messages later in time, but for now, it's OK to apply the "first is worst" principle.

On the next page, you'll see the editor layout and the content of the first welcome message. In this initial welcome message, you noticed that I put placeholder text for the name of our special report, and [LINK] for the link to our eventual welcome page. Later on in this process, we'll go back and create our Welcome page and the special report that goes here.

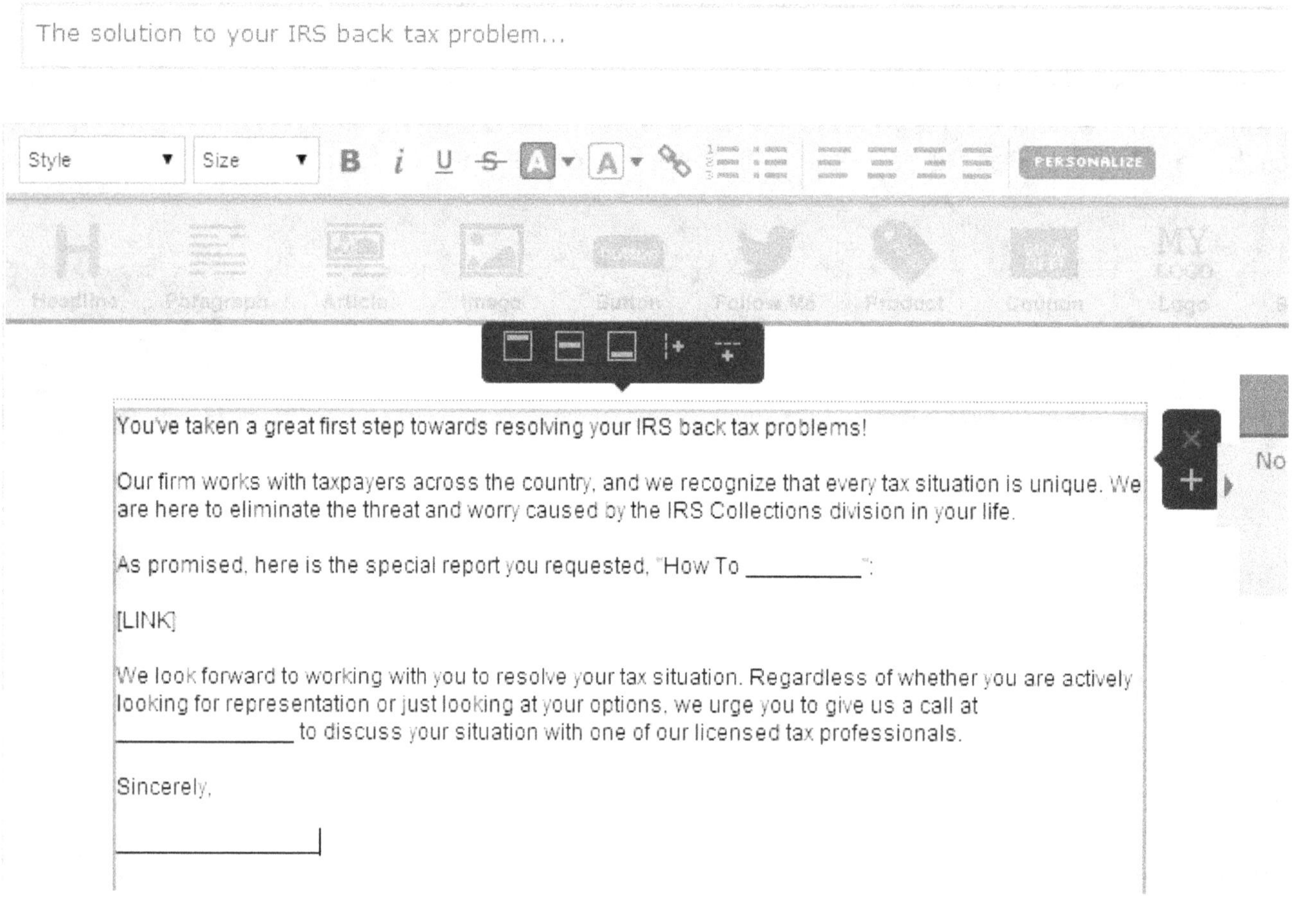

After creating your welcome message, click the green "Next" button at the bottom of the page to be taken to the Settings page.

In the vast majority of situations, you will want to enable click tracking on your follow up messages. We'll discuss this more in a later step, but for now just hit "Save & Exit".

For future reference, you'll add additional follow up messages to this series by clicking the "Create A Follow Up" button, as shown below. For now, however, we need to move on to creating a web form, so we want the button at the bottom of the page for doing this next step.

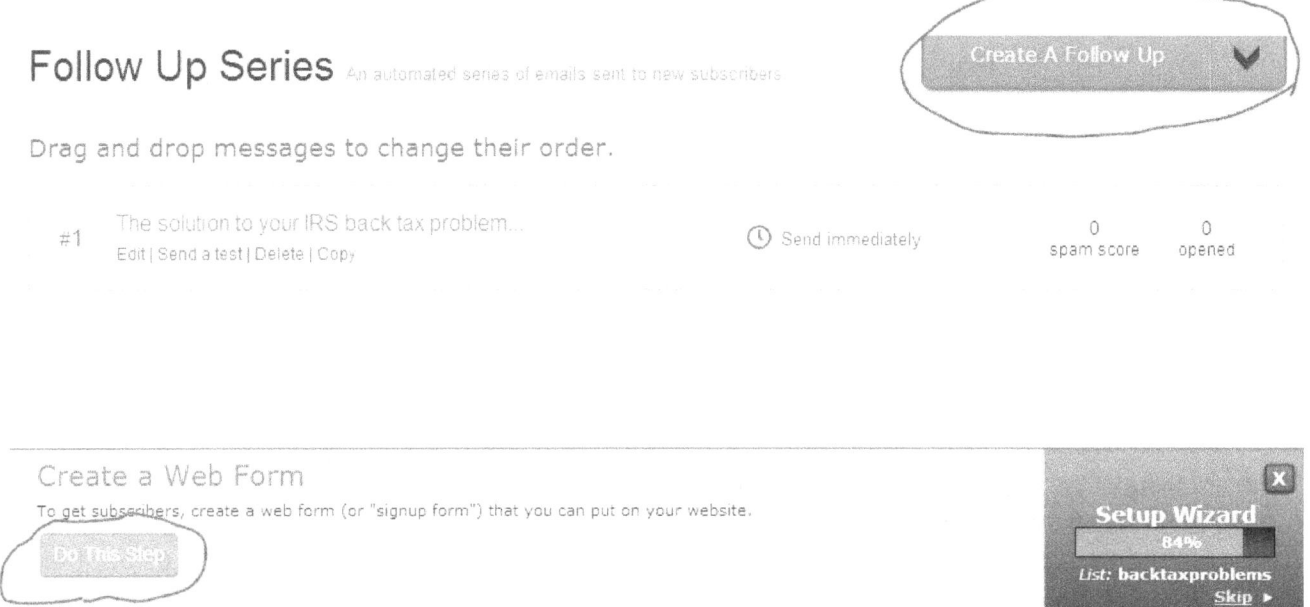

Step 9: Create signup form.

On any site that is dedicated strictly to lead generation, you are looking for one result, and one result only from that site: *For people to step forward and tell you that they're interested in your services.*

That's it. No other goal. The site is not there to service existing clients. It's not there to look pretty. It's only purpose for existing is to deliver leads into your prospect follow up system so that you can nurture those leads over time (which can range from very short to very long) to convert them into paying clients.

With that in mind, we need some way to capture contact information from people that visit the site. In order to do this, we need to create an *offer*. Offers are the core of everything in lead generation. People will only volunteer their contact information if they have a compelling reason to do so. And just in case I haven't stated it frequently enough in other books, articles, and courses: "Free consultation" is not a compelling offer.

I currently have four specific tax resolution lead generation sites such as this one currently operating. These sites are independent of my actual tax firm web site. Each of them is set up exactly like I'm showing you here, and each one uses a different lead magnet to get people's attention and encourage them to provide contact information to me in exchange for receiving information.

One site is aimed at a particular market segment that is only interested in the Offer in Compromise program. For that site, I provide an informative guide to OIC pitfalls. This report is basically one shortened, edited chapter from my *Tax Resolution Secrets* book.

Another site is geared towards people specifically looking for penalty abatement information. For that site, I provide a shortened, edited version of my penalty abatement sample letter kit, which I normally sell for a fee on my tax firm web site.

On yet another site, I discuss at length the pitfalls of the tax resolution industry and provide extensive consumer education on how to avoid being ripped off by the unscrupulous operators in our industry. For this site, I offer consumers a copy of my special report titled *"Five Questions To Ask Any Tax Resolution Firm Before Paying Them A Dime"*. For purposes of this demonstration, I will also use this report on this site. A copy of this report is included in the **Resources** section of this book.

Before discussing the mechanics of creating the actual signup form, a quick word on a very frequently asked question: What to ask for on the form?

Whenever you're doing lead generation, the general suggestion is to ask for the least possible amount of information necessary to get the person into your lead funnel. This makes it as easy as possible for the person to make a decision. The more information you ask for, the fewer people you will have requesting information from you.

It should also be noted that the less information you ask people for, the less qualified the lead is in the short-term. If you ask for a lot of information, such as full name, phone, address, tax debt amount, etc., then the lead is a far more qualified lead in terms of immediacy.
One of my lead generation sites gives away a free copy of my first book, and it is physically shipped to them. Because of this, I ask for full contact information. This site is targeted to higher end tax debtors via direct mail, and I only want highly qualified leads from that site.

In most situations, especially when doing your follow up marketing via email, it is best to ask for the least possible amount of information. For the time being, there is no email tax, so it doesn't cost any extra to email a less qualified lead. Because of this, it's best to collect every lead possible, and let them sift and sort themselves into paying clients based upon the follow messages you send them.

Therefore, for this example site, I'll only be creating forms asking for email addresses. Let's get into the mechanics of that.

When you first enter the sign up form creator in Aweber, you're first taken to the Deisgn screen. The first few times you do this, simply use one of the "Popular" templates. These are the most common and highest converting templates in the Aweber arsenal, so use them for now.

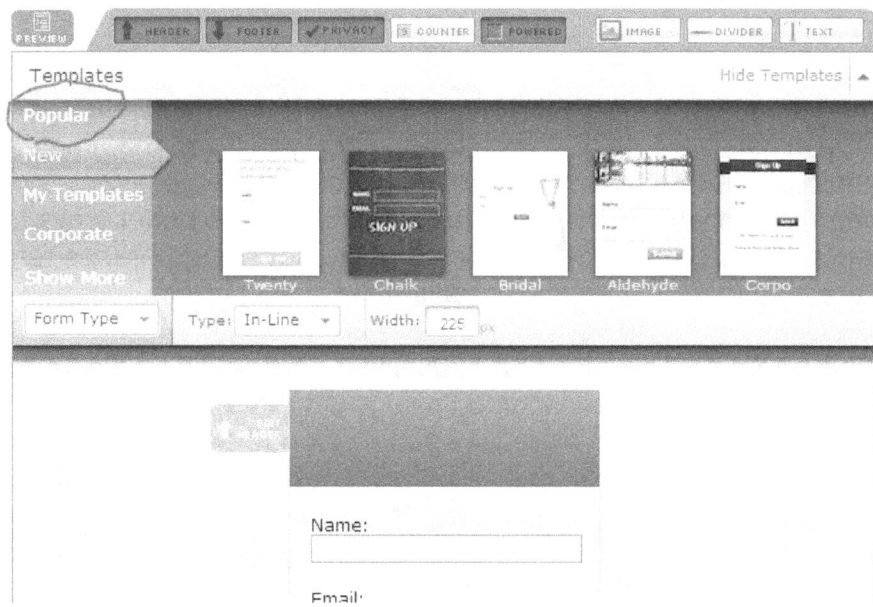

After loading the template, we're going to make some changes. The first thing I'm going to do is remove the "Email" label from the form, and instead include the tag in the box itself. Simply click on the email box itself, and you'll enter the edit mode for that form element. Remove the "Label" text, and enter the "Value" text. You'll also notice that I deleted the "Name" field entirely, and I'll be deleting a few more form fields to heavily simplify this particular form.

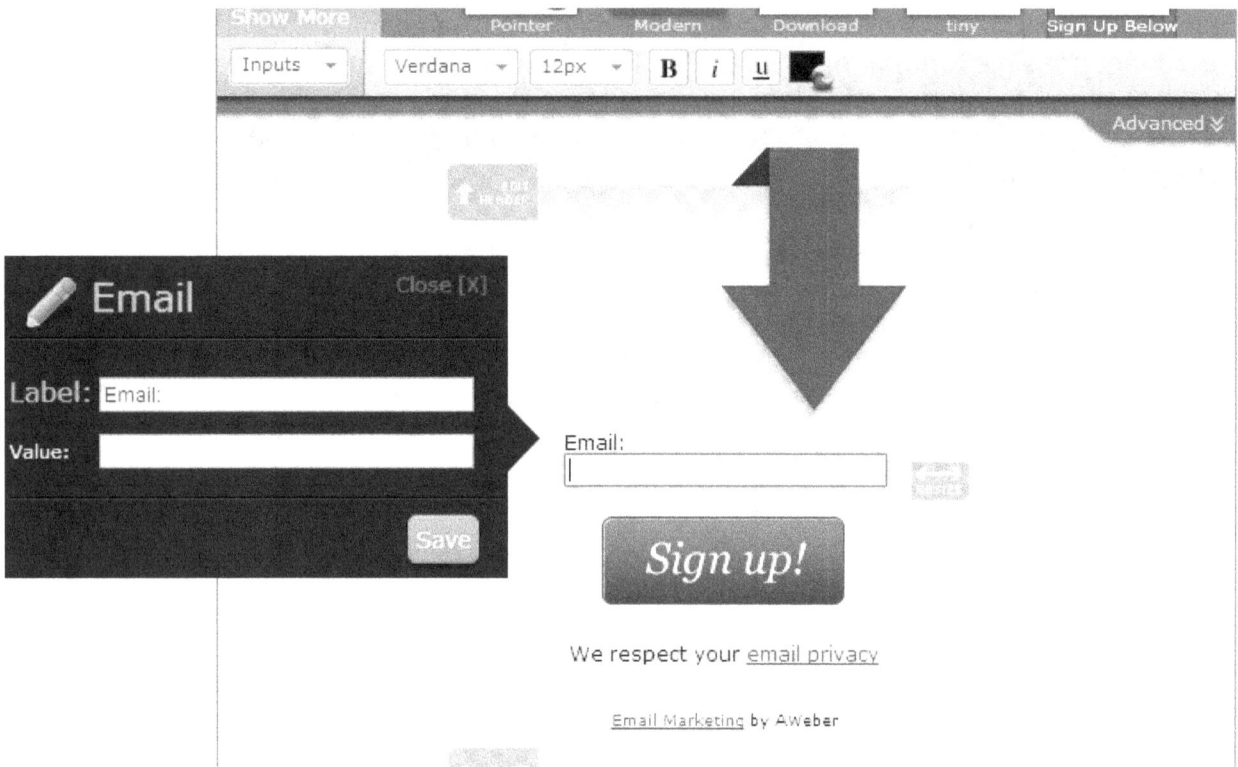

When it comes to form submission buttons, the default "Submit" text is about the worst thing that you can have. In the next screen shot, you'll see that I actually ended up changing the template that I was using, since the first one I selected would not let me change the submit button text (it was an image). There are numerous better ways to say "submit", but years of research has proven that one of the best converting phrases reference the process of getting to the lead magnet that you're having them sign up for.

In this example, I used "Get Access Now", historically a high converting submission button phrase. Note that I also included two greater than signs (>>). Some marketing tests have indicated that this also increases submission rates slightly. I have not seen a difference with this in my own personal testing, but every little thing that could improve response rates should be incorporated when it's this easy to do so.

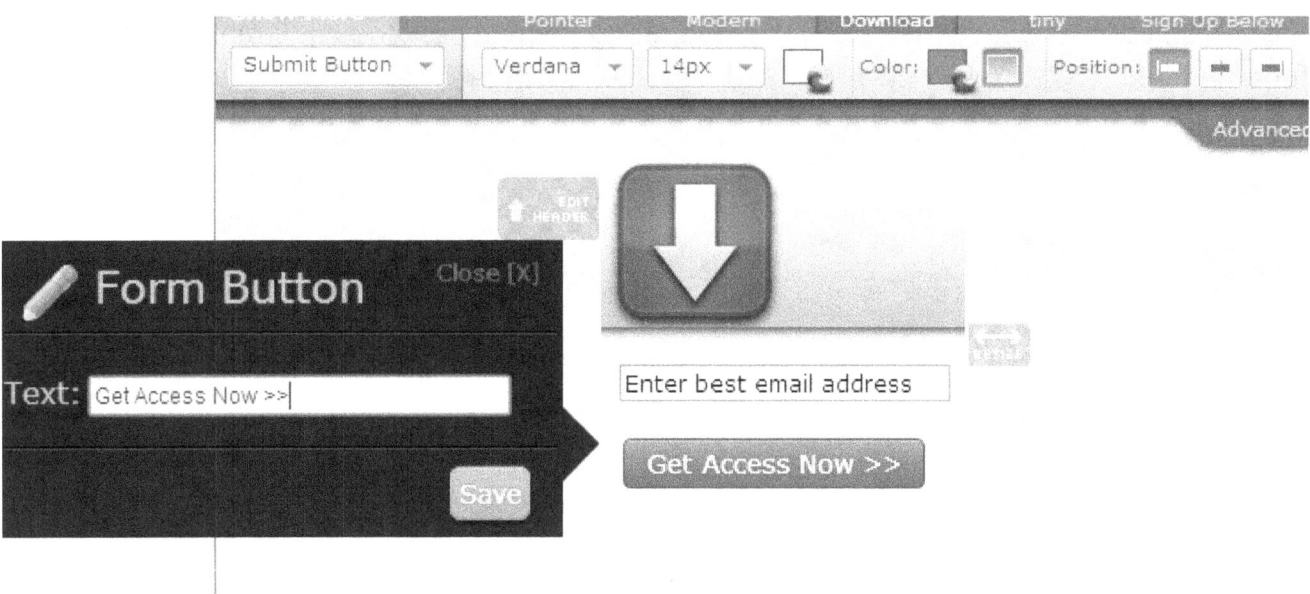

By clicking in the header area next to the area, I'm able to enter the top text that actually tells people what we're offering. Also notice that I deleted the footer and other parts of the form entirely:

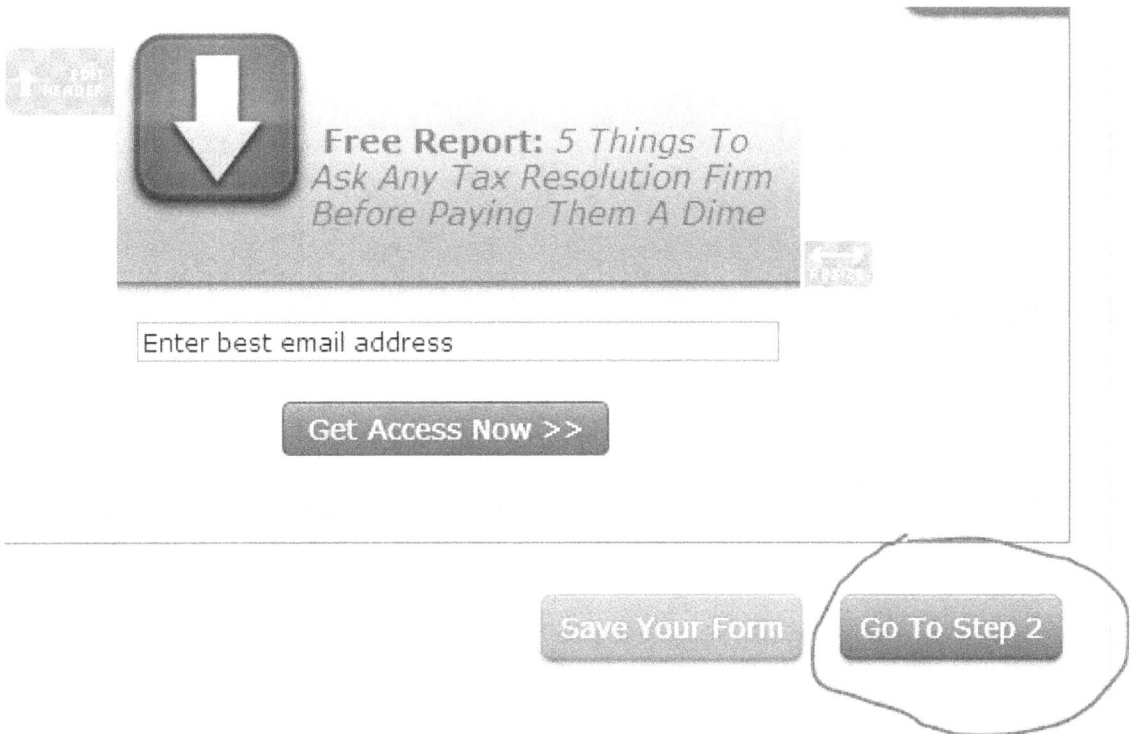

Step 2 of the form creation is the settings. Every form you create should be assigned a unique, descriptive name for tracking purposes. Also, notice that you can choose to have people that sign up redirected to the basic, default Aweber page, or use a custom URL directly on your own site. Eventually, you'll want to create a unique page in your WordPress page where people, commonly a "Thank You" page that instructs them to check their email for the confirmation message that is coming, and telling them to click the confirmation link in that email in order to receive the special report that they are requesting.

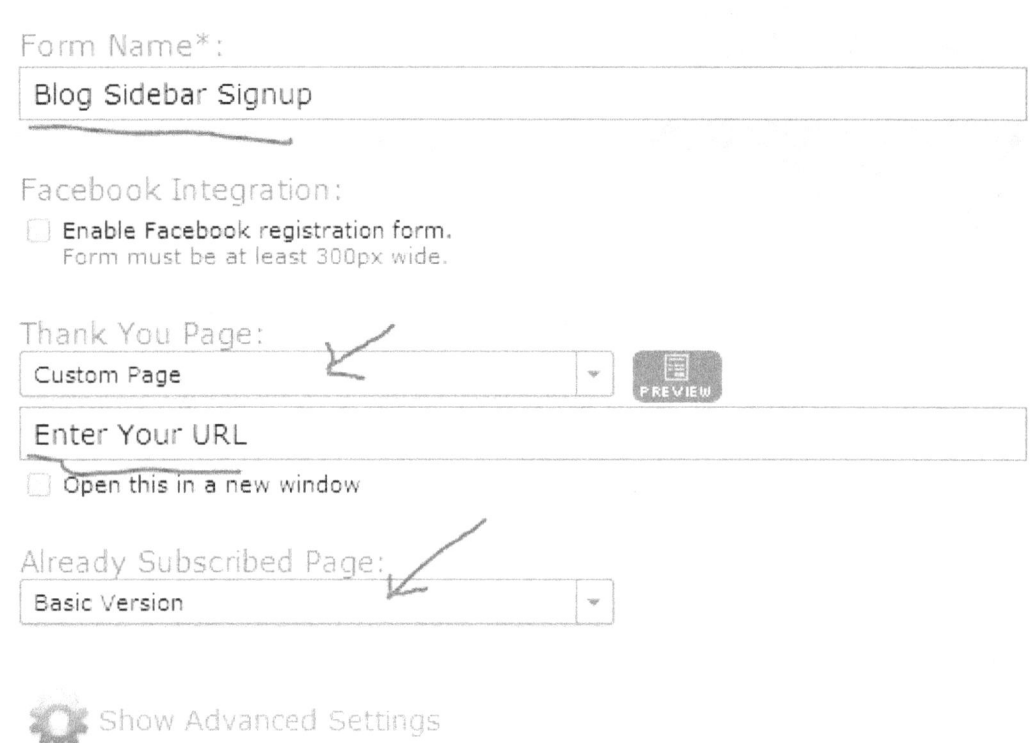

After saving your new form again, you'll be directed to a page that includes the JavaScript code for actually installing your new form.

Who Will Publish This Form To Your Website?

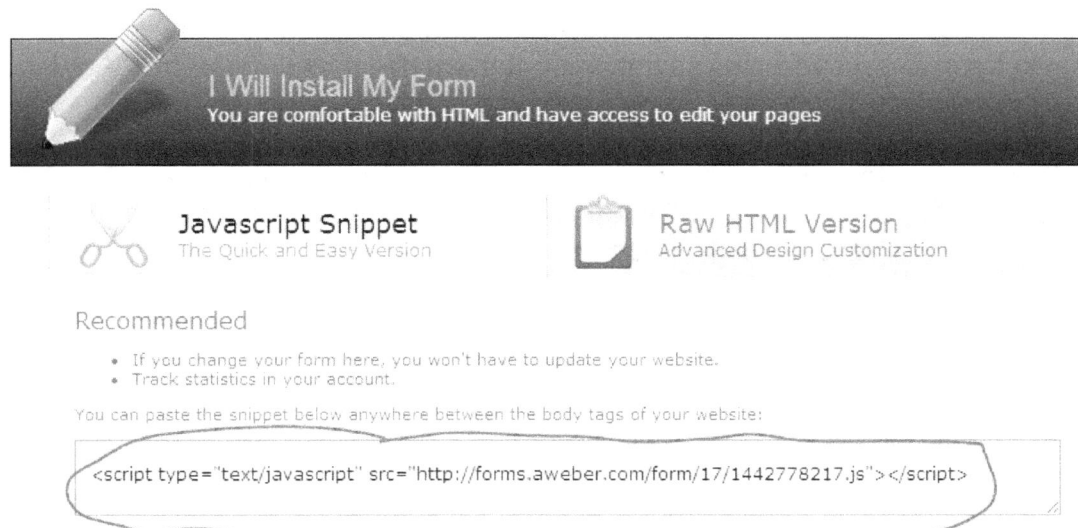

Clicking inside the box circled in red above should automatically highlight the entire code snippet. Copy that to your computer clipboard, because we'll need it for the next step.

TaxMarketingHQ.com

Step 10: Place signup form into WordPress site.

Installing the actual signup form into WordPress is one of the simplest steps of this entire process. Go back to your WordPress administrator interface, and under the "Appearance" tab on the left side, select "Widgets". That will take you to the widget editor page.

What we're going to do now is install a new widget – the Text widget. The text widget is one of the most underrated widgets in all of WordPress, as it allows you to create a movable area of text, HTML, or, in our case, JavaScript code.

To actually install the widget, click your mouse on the Text widget area, circled in red below, and hold your mouse button down while you drag the widget itself over into the sidebar content area of the widget editor.

Recent Comments
Your site's most recent comments.

Recent Posts
Your site's most recent Posts.

RSS
Entries from any RSS or Atom feed.

Search
A search form for your site.

Tag Cloud
A cloud of your most used tags.

Text
Arbitrary text or HTML.

nactive Widgets

Note that you can drag and drop any of the existing widgets in your sidebar to rearrange them. Your sign up box should be the very top widget in any lead generation site you're building. It should always be very visible, even to casual visitors.

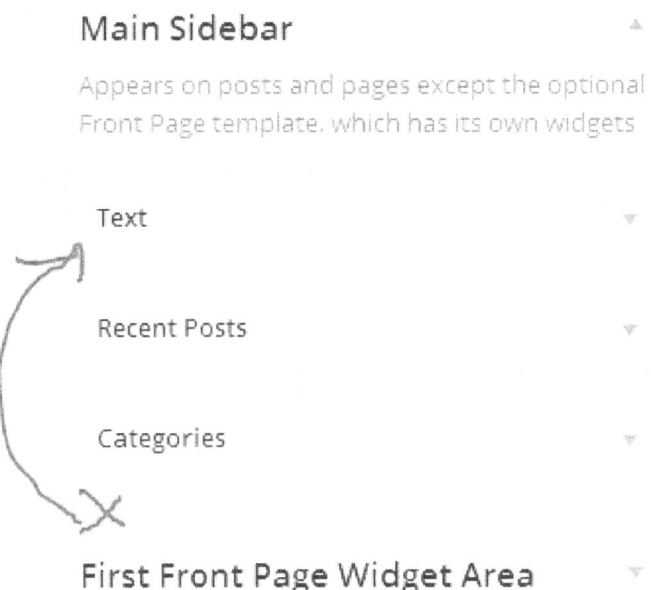

Once you've relocated the widget to the top, click the black triangle at the far right of the widget. This will expand the editor for this particular widget.

Leave the "Title" field blank. Anything you place in the title field will display on the sidebar, and with the particular signup form we're using, we don't need anything in that field. In the big box below the title field, we're going to paste the JavaScript code from Aweber:

After pasting the JavaScript code, press the blue "Save" button.

Step 11: Set up blog post broadcaster.

One of the easiest ways to maintain communication with your new leads, and thus maintain Top of Mind Awareness (TOMA) with them, is to regularly send them your latest blog posts. Since you're going to be creating new blog posts on a regular basis anyway (see step 12) for search engine purposes, you might as well utilize these educational articles to build your relationship with your leads, as well.

If you are subscribed to the *Tax Marketing Tips* newsletter that I send from TaxMarketingHQ.com, then you've seen a blog broadcast system in action. I write my new articles directly inside WordPress, and they are picked up automagically by Aweber and re-formatted into an email to be sent to email subscribers. Here's how that magic works.

First, we need to look up what the web address of our blog's RSS feed is. It's not important for you to have any technical understanding whatsoever about RSS, but it's what makes this whole thing work. By default, any Wordpress installation has an RSS feed accessible by adding "feed" to the end of the web URL, like this:

```
irsbacktaxproblemhelp.com/feed/
```

This XML file does not appear to have any style information associated with it. T]

So whatever your domain name is, simply add /feed/ to the end of it to obtain your WordPress RSS feed URL. Just as a dummy check, enter this URL into your web browser, and verify that you see and XML file warning like the one in the screen shot above.

For us, our feed URL is http://IRSBackTaxProblemHelp.com/feed/

Now that we have this, we can create a Blog Broadcast in Aweber. To access the editor for this, go back to your Aweber admin interface, click "Messages", then click "Blog Broadcast" from the Messages sub-menu.

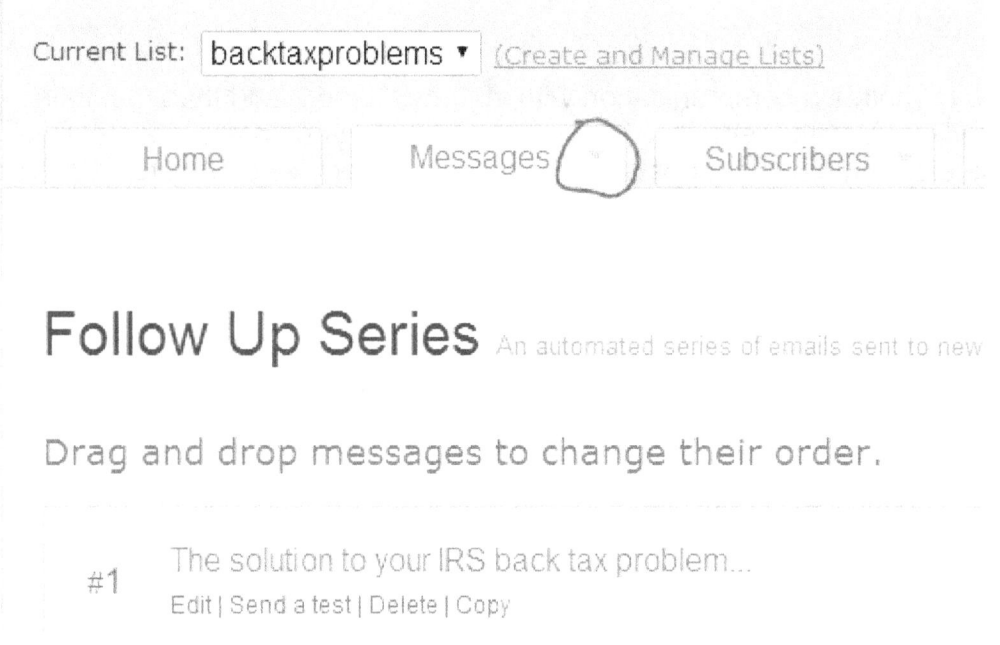

On the Blog Broadcast page, hit the green button to create a new one:

This will put you into the message editor. It's basically the same message editor you've already used, with a couple differences. You'll need to paste in the RSS feed URL that we already found, plus enter a default subject line for the emails. Note that all the emails sent will use this same subject line, but there is a nifty trick that Aweber gives us that lets us use the blog post title as the subject line.

In the editor, note that I have not loaded a template on the right side. I'm using the "Basic Plain Template". I suggest sticking with this one for pretty much all intents and purposes. Never forget that our purpose here has nothing to do with looking pretty or being fancy. We are not selling graphic design services – "pretty" does not win us points with leads, and can actually work against us.

So what's the subject line trick? It's a special code that Aweber lets us use to rip out part of the RSS feed and use just a specific part of the XML stream in a particular location. Didn't follow that? No worries, just put this in the subject line:

{!rss_itemblock}{!rss_item_title}{!rss_itemblockend}

See the part there that says rss_item_title? That's what we're doing: Just using the title.

If you want to use some sort of identifier tag in your emails, it is common to precede the subject line with this. An example subject line might look like this:

[Back Taxes] The 5 most common tax debt mistakes people make

If you want to use such a tag, and have every email go out with the [Back Taxes] tag, simply add it like this in the blog broadcast editor:

[Back Taxes] {!rss_itemblock}{!rss_item_title}{!rss_itemblockend}

It's important to understand that every email sent using the blog broadcaster will look exactly the same. You're creating an email template here, and information from your blog posts will be inserted into this template.

For the message body, we want to include the rss_item_description element from the RSS feed, as shown below:

```
Plain Text Message:

{!rss_itemblock} {!rss_item_description} {!rss_itemblockend}

Sincerely,

_____
```

Here's the code block in a copyable format:

{!rss_itemblock} {!rss_item_description} {!rss_itemblockend}

In almost all of my blog broadcast setups, I'll include a P.S. with an offer and a call to action. I will change this occasionally to prevent it from getting sterile, or to reflect what I'm currently doing. For example, during periods of time when I want to ramp up and get more tax clients, I might include an invitation to a free webinar. During time periods when I'm not actively seeking clients, such as last month when I was in Europe, I might change it to a book offer, linking directly to the Amazon product page for my consumer tax resolution book.

At the bottom of the editor screen, there is a "Next" button that will take us to the settings page for the blog broadcaster.

In general, it's best to send all blog broadcasts "immediately", when the number of new items is simply "1". Since we're trying to create an automated sales funnel here, also be sure to click the "Send Automatically" toggle. Then, click "Save Blog Broadcast".

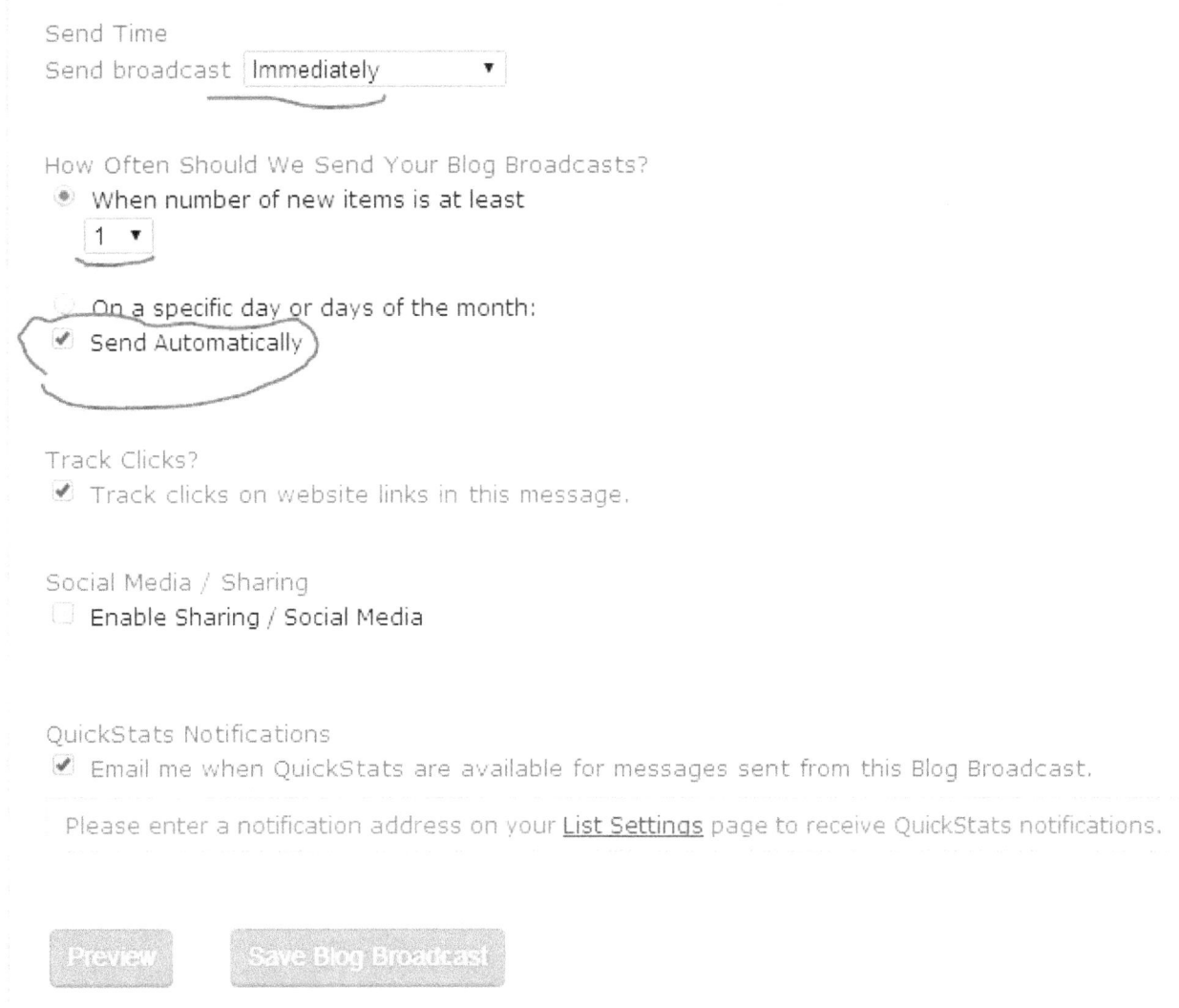

This completes the blog broadcast setup process, and you'll see your new blog broadcast in the list thereof.

Note that you can actually create more than one blog broadcaster in Aweber for each list. You can have as many as you want, actually. Why would you want to do this? Perhaps you want email subscribers to receive all new blog posts from BOTH this lead generation site, but also your primary firm web site. If you run two separate blogs, with different content, there is no harm in sending copies of both articles to your leads.

Blog Broadcast
Convert your latest blog posts into a newsletter.

Blog Title	Last Checked	Send Automatically
IRS Back Tax Problem Help	04/08/14 4:33pm	Yes

Here are those RSS segment snippets again in one place for easy copy/paste into Aweber:

Subject: {!rss_itemblock}{!rss_item_title}{!rss_itemblockend}

Body: {!rss_itemblock} {!rss_item_description} {!rss_itemblockend}

Step 12: Create an editorial schedule.

You may be wondering why we're setting this whole thing up on a blog, instead of just using a simple page that just offers our lead magnet in exchange for our lead's contact information. The reason has to do with how people get to the web site in the first place.

According to data firm FactBrowser, business to business marketers (that's us) who use blogs generate 67% more leads per month than those who don't. It should also be noted that bloggers that post frequently enjoy much higher search engine rankings than those that do not.

In short, Google and other search engines reward sites that provide visitors with recent, updated information. Particularly when it comes to ever-changing tax laws, our leads are going to be seeking the latest information available that applies to their problem. In order to deliver updated information, we are going to create a regular schedule for adding new posts to our new blog, and we are going to select our topics in advance so that we don't need to think about it every time we sit down to write (this is a time management and "*getting things done*" tactic). In the journalism world, such an advance written plan for what to publish and when is called an **editorial calendar**.

There are a number of ways to create an editorial calendar for yourself. Of course, you can just put it on your personal calendar: Make a standing appointment with yourself once a week for 15, 30, 60 minutes – however much time you need to create a good quality piece of written content.

I'd suggest taking it a step further, however. WordPress gives you the ability to schedule when a post is published on your blog. This allows you to write posts well in advance of when they need to actually appear. You don't even need to write the entire post: You can simply save it with a title and a blank body, and schedule the post for some time in the future.

In the WordPress post editor, on the right hand side, is where you set the date and time:

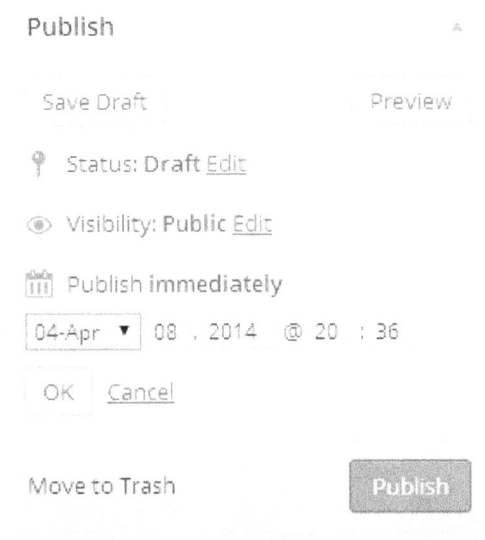

By creating and scheduling at least your post titles, you create a placeholder that you can go back to. It becomes far less daunting of a task during your scheduled writing time to create a new article if at least the title and topic are selected ahead of time.

Another tactic that you can use is to batch your blog posting. In batching, you write more than one complete post at a time, and schedule them for future release. Batching allows you to take advantage of particularly creative periods of time, when writer's block isn't an issue.

No matter how you approach it, it is essential for you to create an editorial calendar and <u>stick to it</u>. You should aim to post new articles on this blog at least every other week. If you are not going to create the post drafts ahead of time and schedule them for the future, then you should at least schedule the time for yourself to write, and create a list of topics to write about. As you write each article in the future, remove it from the list.

This is actually my preferred method. I have extensive lists of article topics in different categories. For example, you could maintain a list of article topics for tax planning, one for 1040 returns, another for wealth management, another for tax resolution, etc.

Here is a sample topic list for tax debt resolution:

- Understanding IRS Collection Financial Standards
- How To Obtain A Guaranteed Installment Agreement
- Eligibility Requirements For Streamline Installment Agreements
- The Express Path To In-Business Installment Agreements
- The Truth About "Pennies On The Dollar"
- Why Your Tax Store Preparer Can't Represent You
- Understanding IRS Deadlines – And What Happens When You Ignore Them
- Health Issues? Get Your IRS Penalties Waived
- Never Give Up: What To Do When The IRS Tells You "No"
- How To Remove IRS Wage Garnishments
- How To Buy A New Home When You Have A Federal Tax Lien
- Your Spouse's Tax Problem Doesn't Need To Be Your Problem
- NEVER Sign Anything From The IRS Without Doing This First
- Is bankruptcy an option for your tax debts?
- What Your IRS Notice Actually Means
- Yes, The IRS Really Can Personally Stick You With A Business Tax Bill

These were literally just off the top of my head during a 5-minute brainstorming session. Taking the time to brainstorm a list like this for yourself, and keeping it handy during your writing sessions, will make the process of crafting your new blog posts much easier.

A brief word about writing... Some tax professionals reading this manual might be having a slight panic attack at the thought of having to write. Most people don't think that they have the ability to write very well, and are almost as afraid of writing as they are of public speaking.

The best advice I can provide on this topic is to simply not worry about it. I know that's easy to say, and harder to practice. When it comes to writing articles for your blog, they do not have to be perfect. In fact, it's better if they're not. When you're writing your articles, I'd encourage you to just pretend that you are writing a quick email to a client. Whatever topic you're writing about, rephrase it into the form of a question, and respond to it using a conversational style just like you would in a private email.

For example, let's take a random one from my list above: What Your IRS Notice Actually Means.

While we'd stick with that as the article title, let's rephrase it into a question to make it easier to address for us from a conversational standpoint. For example, think of it this way:

Hey, this week in the mail I received two letters from the IRS, and I have no idea what they mean. One of them is labeled CP-504 in the bottom right corner, and the other is labeled a Letter 1058. They're both talking about "levies". I'm kind of worried. What are these? Do I need to do anything? And why are they somewhat different but talking about the same thing?

Pretending that this was an email from a client, and responding appropriately, makes the writing process far easier for most people. With this approach, you need not worry about how long to make the article, or what specific things you need to touch on: You're simply responding to the "email inquiry".

When writing blog posts, do NOT:

- Be concerned about word count.
- Worry about perfect grammar.
- Being perfectly polished and professional
- Think about keyword phrases and other things you may hear about SEO.

Simply write a conversational email to a client. That's it. Cover the topic adequately, and end EVERY post with a clear call to action: An invitation to call for an appointment, an evaluation, a free report, etc.

The most important part of your editorial calendar is creating something you can live with. Whether this is pre-scheduling post drafts directly in WordPress, or once a month writing four or five full length articles for the future, or working 30 minutes weekly from a topic idea list – pick the method that works best for you and that will enable you to get it done.

Shameless Plug: All Tax Marketing HQ Diamond members receive two pre-written articles each month to be used in their client newsletters, email autoresponders, or as blog posts. When using these articles as blog posts, it is highly encouraged that you rewrite to a significant extent, in order to avoid Google's infamous *duplicate content penalty*. Even with the necessity of the editing, however, these articles are a great starting point for your blog posting each month. If you are already a Diamond member and are not using these, you can find them in your members area. New articles are posted roughly mid-month, each and every month. If you are not yet a Diamond member, you can learn more here:

http://taxmarketinghq.com/diamond

Step 13: Upload report and add link to email.

You'll remember that when we created the first welcome message in our email autoresponder system, I left a blank space to insert the link to the actual report for our lead to download. We're going to fix that now. In addition, we need to create our Welcome page that confirmed subscribers go to.

The easiest way to do this is to use the built in WordPress media uploader to insert our special report into the Welcome page, and simply use the welcome page as the link in our first follow up message.

Before we create the Welcome page and update our first autoresponder message, we need to create the PDF for the special report itself. I'll do this in Microsoft Word, which has a very convenient "Save to PDF" feature.

First I'll copy and paste the special report from the **Resources** section of this manual into a new Word document:

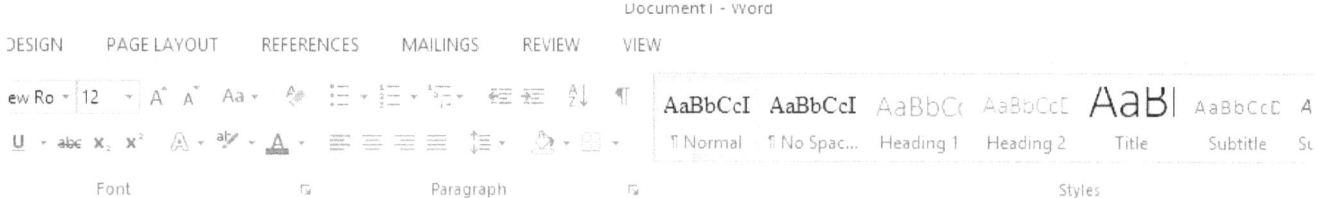

Whenever you copy and paste from a PDF document such as this manual, it isn't going to look very pretty. Therefore, some formatting is going to be required to make it look nice:

Notice that I added the "Presented by your friends" bit at the top, and included a phone number. This helps set the precedent for your helpful, available nature – there whenever they need you.

Note: My apologies in advance if "Taxes-R-Us" is somebody's actual company name. It was intended tongue-in-cheek for illustrative purposes.

At the end of the document, I'm also going to add a strong call to action. Notice that the call to action is very specific – directing them to perform one action only. Also note that it offers them something in writing, and is worded to address the concerns raised with the five questions in the report. You'll quickly notice that the "Tax Debt Settlement Analysis" offer is, essentially, a free consultation, but:

1. I don't call it that.
2. It's packaged differently.
3. They *receive* something in the end.

If you're following along with the terminology, also note that when they actually call and request the consultation, errrmmmm, I mean, "Tax Debt Settlement Analysis", this *lead* has officially converted into a *prospect*.

Lastly, be sure that anything and everything you discuss with a tax resolution firm, such as fees, covered services, responsibilities, deadlines, etc., are all in WRITING. Don't sign a contract, and definitely don't give them your credit card number without seeing everything in writing first.

Armed with these questions, you should be better positioned to make a wise decision regarding hiring professional tax services.

Need help now?

At Taxes-R-Us, we take your tax situation seriously, even if our name isn't. Call us right now at (212) 555-5555 and ask to speak with one of our licensed, experienced tax debt resolution professionals. You will be connected to an actual taxpayer representative that is experienced in working with the IRS – not a salesperson. Be sure to mention our **Tax Debt Settlement Analysis** offer, and your licensed specialist will provide you with a written evaluation of your tax situation, and helpful guidance for resolving your tax problem. This analysis and written evaluation are yours FREE just for calling. Call us right now at (212) 555-5555 for your complimentary evaluation.

Now that I'm done with the report, I'm going to save it as a PDF. In order to do this in Word, select the "File" menu, then "Save as…". Select your destination folder on your computer, and select the "Save type as" to "PDF":

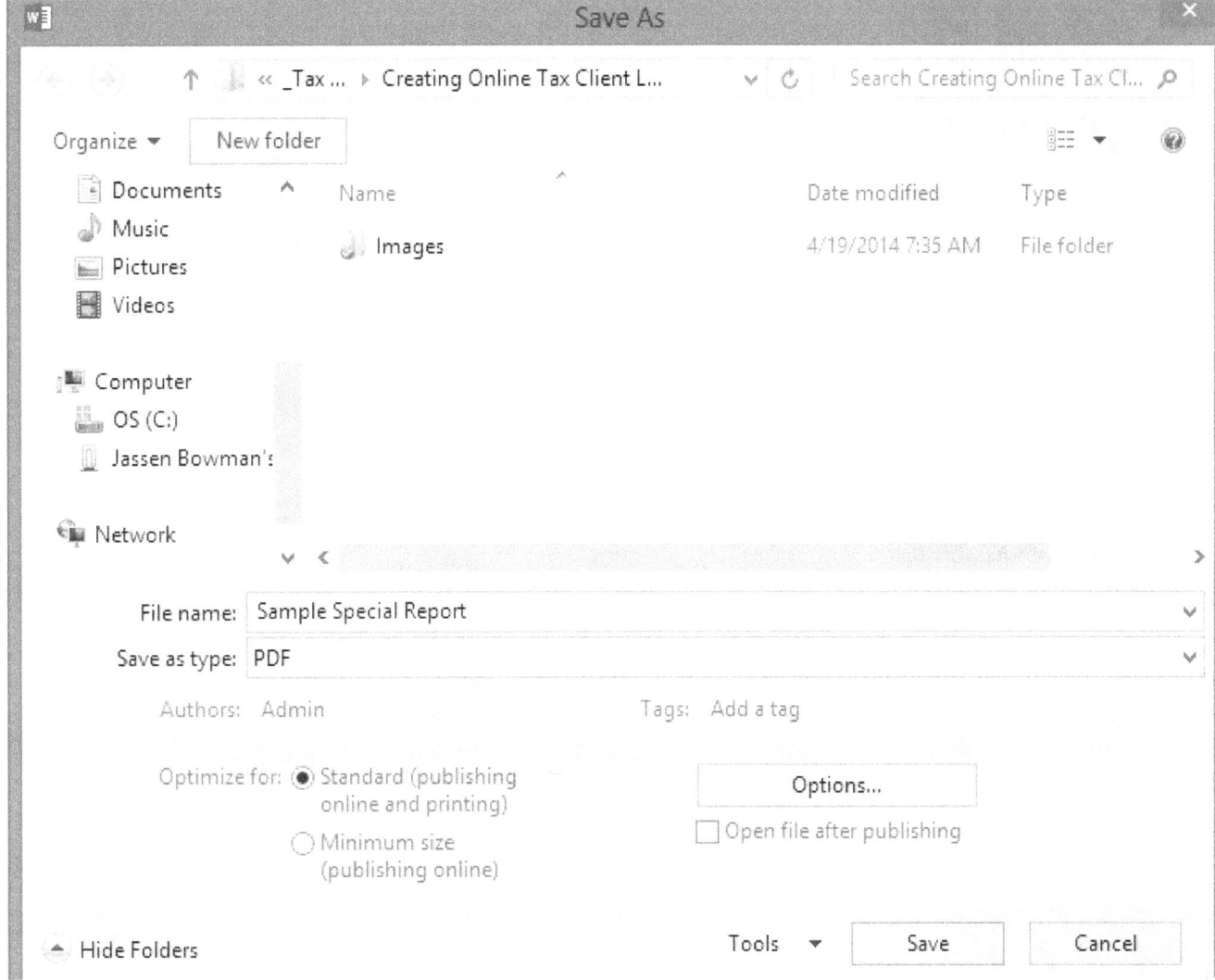

This PDF is then what we will upload to WordPress. With that in mind, let's now create our "Welcome" page on the blog itself, which is where we will both automatically redirect people that click the confirmation link in the confirmation email, and also the link we will include in the first welcome message.

In WordPress, create a new PAGE. It is important to note the distinction between posts and pages here – we want a page, not a post.

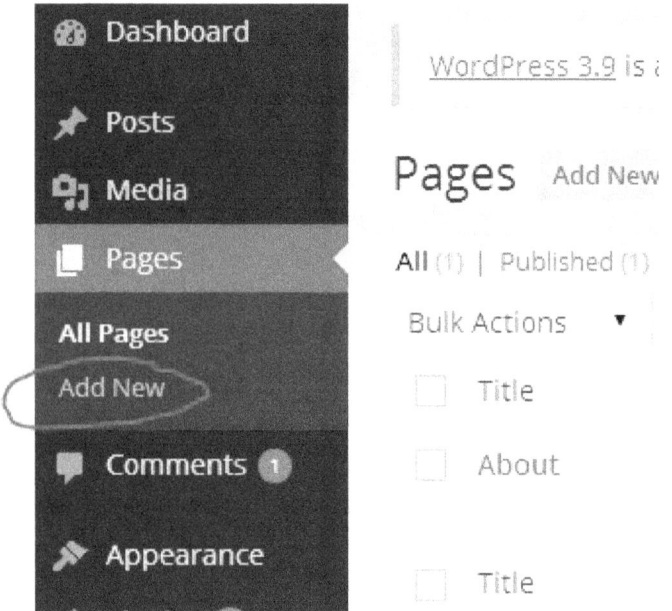

We're going to, appropriately, call this page, "Welcome". If we leave it simply as "Welcome", the permalink to it will also just be /welcome, which is important because we've already told Aweber that this is the place to send people after they confirm their request for information from us.

On our new page, we're now going to use the media uploader to insert our special report.

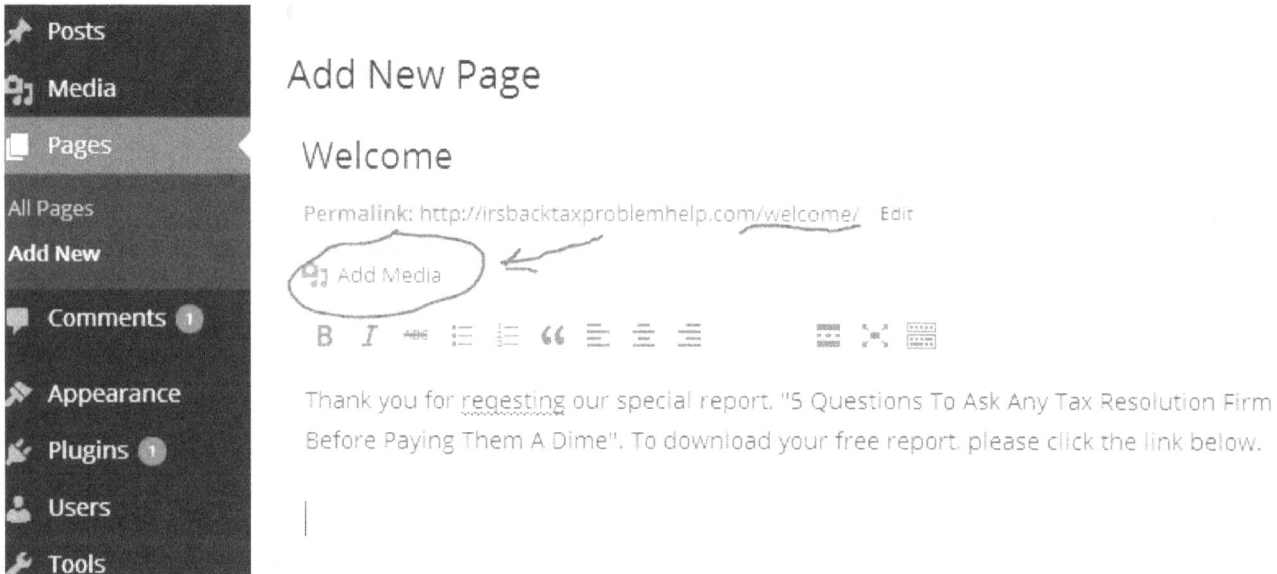

Click the "Add Media" button to be taken to the media uploader….

Insert Media

Upload Files   Media Library

Drop files anywhere to upload

Select Files

Maximum upload file size: 64MB.

The easiest way to insert the file is to drag and drop it from the location you saved the PDF on your hard drive. Alternatively, you can select "Select Files" and a dialog box will open and you can find and select the file. Once uploaded….

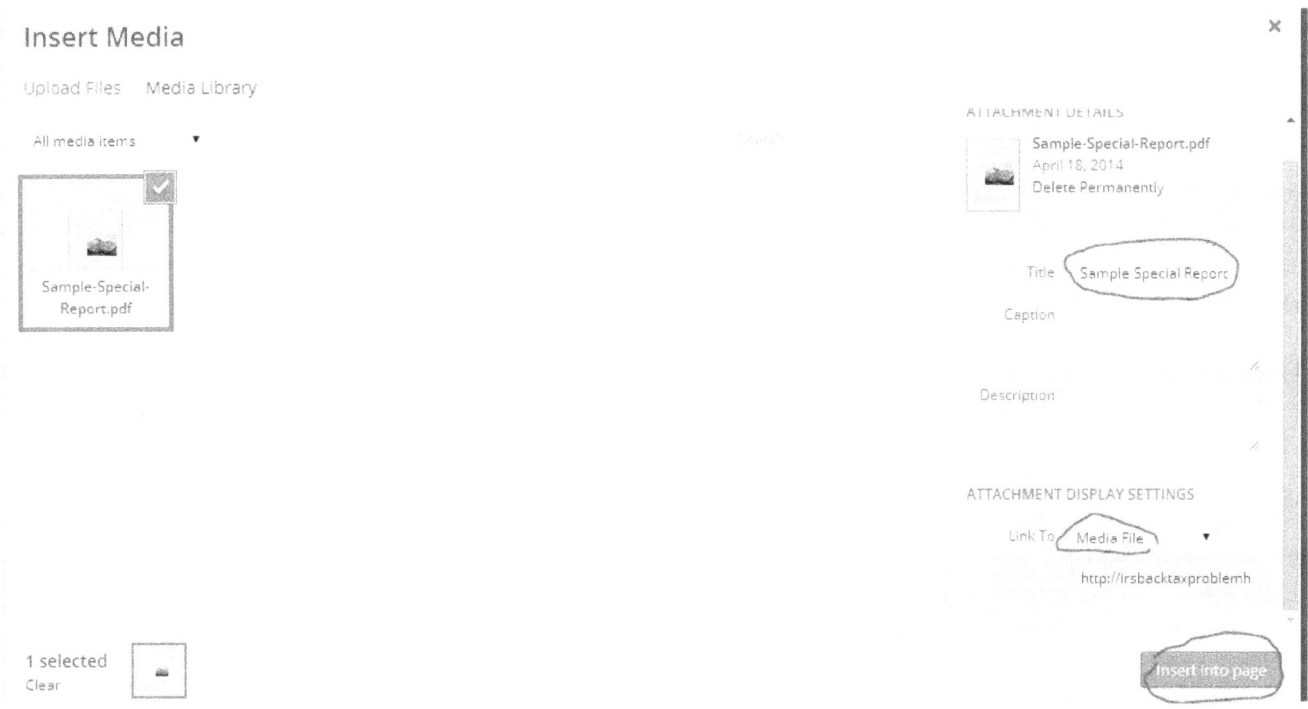

You can edit the title of the report as used within Wordpress. Be sure the "Link To" says *media file*, and then click insert into page, which will insert the actual link to the PDF file:

Add New Page

Welcome

Permalink: http://irsbacktaxproblemhelp.com/welcome/ Edit

Add Media

Thank you for reqesting our special report, "5 Questions To Ask Any Tax Resolution Firm Before Paying Them A Dime". To download your free report, please click the link below.

Sample Special Report

Should you be in immediate need of assistance with your tax debt issue, please call us at _____ for your no cost, no obligation *Tax Debt Settlement Analysis*. We will provide you with a written evaluation of your tax problem, and provide guidance on how to resolve your situation.

Notice that the link to the PDF file shows up using the title we gave it in the media uploader. Also note that I repeated the call to action from the special report directly on the welcome page. **Your call to action that converts leads to prospects should be repeated everywhere that the lead engages with you.**

The next thing for us to do is actually "Publish" this page, so that it is publicly displayed. After that, we need to add the link to this page into our welcome message in the autoresponder.

Note: With some WordPress themes, including the default themes, new Pages are automatically added to your main site navigation. You don't want people to access the report without signing up for it, so if the WordPress theme you choose automatically adds the "Welcome" page to the main site menu, be sure to go into the Menus editor, toggle the page info, and select "Remove" to delete it.

To edit our autoresponder welcome message, login to the email system, select the email list, and under the "Messages" tab select "Follow Up" messages. Doing this will put us on this page:

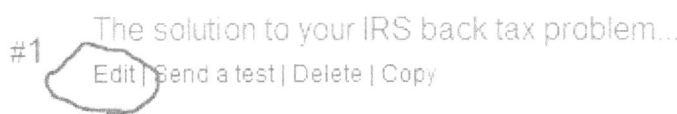

Now click the "Edit" link underneath the message title to be taken to the editor. Within the editor, we are going to add a hyperlink to our new Welcome page. We had previously put in a place holder text that said [LINK], so we can now delete that and add the real link. Be sure the cursor inside the editor box is in the right place where you want the link to appear, and then click the chain link icon near the top of the editor:

This will bring up a new box where you will type or paste the URL to our welcome page. For our demo site, that URL was http://irsbacktaxproblemhelp.com/welcome.

After inserting the new link, click "Next" at the bottom of the editor. On the next page are the settings for this message. While it is generally best to enable click tracking on links in your emails, it's also not a good idea to have emails show up to people's inboxes that contain garbled links. For welcome emails in particular, I want people to actually see the URL they are going to, as part of building trust with the new lead. Because of this, I want the actual URL to show up, not the garbled tracking URL. Thus, I am going to disable click tracking here:

Then click "Save & Exit", and…….**WE'RE DONE!!!** ☺

Traffic Precedes Leads

In the exact same way that a retail store location needs people walking in the door, often called "foot traffic", your shiny new lead generation web site is useless without *web traffic*.

Obtaining web traffic can be a massive, and expensive, undertaking. However, application of the 80/20 rule shows us that we can get the majority of the results, without doing ALL of the work. The 80/20 rule is critical to my entire lead generation automation strategy, to be honest, since I do all of this stuff for my own practice entirely myself (for current lifestyle design considerations, I have zero employees at the moment).

From the perspective of our funnel analogy, *traffic* is what we put into the top of our funnel. With traffic, we have eyeballs on our site. Traffic represents people with a problem that found our site through one means or another, people that we can present our lead magnet to.

So how do we get traffic? Basically, *any way that we can!*

In broad terms, we will usually drive traffic via online and offline means. Offline means of driving traffic might include:

- Radio spots
- TV commercials
- Newspaper ads
- Highly targeted direct mail (my personal favorite)

Offline marketing strategies are beyond the scope of this particular manual, as here we are concerned about online tactics. Online tactics will generally be broken down into free and paid methods.

Even though it's not technically proper to do so, I lump all my free traffic tactics together into my search engine optimization (SEO) strategy. There are pieces of this SEO strategy that don't actually contribute to search engine placement, per se, but they are important free online methods for attracting visitors that they are included in the most appropriate place.

When it comes to paid traffic, my entire 80/20 strategy right now is about one thing: Facebook ads. While it could be argued that paid LinkedIn ads are also appropriate for finding business tax clients, I have not tested this, and at the time being feel it would fall out of the 20% rule as an outlier. Why not Google Adwords, I hear some people asking? Simply because Google Adwords has become grossly overpriced in relation to the ROI.

The next two sections will describe in detail my 80/20 SEO strategy, and what you need to know to run Facebook ad campaigns.

The Pareto SEO Strategy

The concept of "minimum effective dose" has been widely popularized by startup guru Tim Ferriss, author of the *4-Hour* series of books. This concept, very closely related to the Pareto Principle (the 80/20 rule), seeks to find the bare minimum amount of X required to produce desired result Y.

The vast majority of information available on the subject of search engine marketing is extremely convoluted, complicated, and excessively over-excessive, and often repetitively redundant (…see what I did there?). On top of that, a lot of the information circling the Internet marketing blogs and forums is simply either wrong or heavily frowned upon by the search engines that you're trying to impress. Some of these tactics are referred to as "black hat" techniques; most of us just call it *spam* (link spam, video spam, comment spam, forum spam…it's all just spam).

The entire goal of all your SEO/SEM efforts is simple: **Get interested eyeballs onto your web site.** That's it, that's the entire goal of SEO/SEM. Once they're actually on your web site, that's when your sales funnel kicks in and you convert visitors to leads.

I want to point out that, from a practical standpoint, all of the following terms *mean the exact same thing*:

- Search Engine Optimization (SEO)
- Search Engine Marketing (SEM)
- Article Marketing
- Content Marketing
- Traffic Building
- Video Marketing
- Backlink Building

There are definitely Internet marketing purists that will call me out and say, "No, those are all different." They can scream that all they want, but no, they're wrong. The specific media mode that you use to get organic search traffic to your site may vary, but the end result is all the same.

I use the term SEO simply because I've been around for a while, and it was one of the earliest terms applied to the process of intentionally doing things to get more web traffic from search engines, but it's still all under the same umbrella.

So, hopefully we can all agree that the end goal is the same, no matter how we do it: **Get people from the search engines to us.**

Despite the endless rhetoric online about the "this and that" of SEO, modern SEO really only boils down to three requirements:

1. Be listed (where it matters most).
2. Be published (where it matters).
3. Be engaged (with your prospects and clients).

Let's briefly talk about the search engines themselves. I'm going to stop saying *the search engines*, because the basic reality of search is that only one search engine even matters. Google is the single most heavily used search engine on the Internet, and YouTube is #2…and YouTube is owned by Google. So, the focus is on Google and their algorithm.

A discussion about doing Pareto SEO isn't complete without mentioning a heavily discussed topic: Google's occasional algorithm updates. If you've ever been *Google slapped*, then you know what I'm referring to. The key thing to remember about every major algorithm change that Google makes is that these algorithm changes are made to reduce the impact of spammy SEO activities.

When Google engineers identify some loophole in their algorithm that people are exploiting to rank higher, they fix that loophole in order to make the search results more relevant and accurate.

This concept is important, because it heavily impacts the tactics we engage in to achieve minimal (and lasting) SEO. In the three years I've been operating my niche authority sites, **I have never once had my rankings go down because of a Google algorithm change**. In fact, I often get *boosts* in the SERPs (Search Engine Results Pages) because Google does me a favor by eliminating the useless *crap* that other people add to their index.

Things I Don't Do

There are some common things I do NOT do, and do NOT recommend that you do:

1. Link wheels. Google is super-smart, and can identify "footprints" such as those left by automated link wheels. Same with link pyramids.

2. Forum spamming. Some people spam forums in order to get their links (usually via forum signatures) out there. Don't bother. These are usually removed by the forum owners, and are often no-follow links.

3. Blog spamming. Some people leave comments on blog posts for no other reason than to try and get a link. Don't waste your time. Most are no-follow, most spam comments are never posted, and Google can detect this behaviour.

4. Web 2.0 profile spam. This is kind of a new one to me, but apparently some people create massive numbers of profile on various web 2.0 and social media sites, and put links to things in there. This is also trackable by Google, and while it may get you short-term SEO boosts now, it'll be corrected by Google in a future algorithm update, if they haven't already.

Bottom line here: **Don't spam, in any form**.

Be Listed

You can spend countless hours studying SEO. Most SEO strategies rely on getting links to your site from other sites, as this is still a significant portion of most search algorithms. SEO books, courses, articles, and videos will provide you literally thousands of different recommendations on how to get backlinks, and where to get them from.

In reality, most of that backbreaking backlink building is a waste of time. In some cases, the advice is straight up rubbish, and will actually do more harm than good. Google can, has, and will ban sites from their index when you use "black hat" tactics, or make it too obvious that you're trying to game the system.

The reality is that you can perform extremely well in the search engine results by having a very small number of backlinks. What's important is that the links to you are from relevant sources. For example, a link to an article on your blog from a Forbes.com contributor is worth far more to you than thousands of spammy backlinks from crappy sites that no humans actually visit. Some experts have stated that one single link from a quality, authority site can be worth 50,000 to 100,000 crap/spam links from all other sources.

Why? Because you're a business and financial professional, and Forbes is a business and financial site. Not only that, it's one of the biggest and most respected such sites, so a link from Forbes carries significant "link juice".

How do you get a link from Forbes? Easy: Write an article for them, or contact one of their contributing writers and share a statistic or sound bite for them to include in an article.

How Backlinks Work

Obtaining keyword-anchored links to the content on your web site is the single most important component of boosting your search engine positioning. The link text (the actual text you click on in a link) is usually a keyword phrase that you found that you want to link for. Google, as well as other search engines, counts the number of links from other web sites to yours as "votes" for the authority of your web site. The more links back to your site with your selected keyword as the link text, the higher your site will rank in the search engines.

There are hundreds of other factors that SEO professionals work on in order to boost your search engine position, but this is a situation where the Pareto Principle definitely applies.

The search engines do not reveal their exact algorithms, of course, but experts have demonstrated that approximately 70% of the results obtained in their SEO efforts is directly related to their backlink strategies.

The best way to get backlinks to your web site is the natural way: People find a piece of content on your web site, then link to it in something they write on their own web site.

Getting a large number of links this way, however, is not very fast. Unless your web site is already popular and has lots of visitors that share your content with others, this is unlikely to happen. It's also a horrible idea to use any of the automated software services that purport to generate hundreds and thousands of backlinks, as Google has explicitly declared that use of such tools will simply get your site banned by Google (and yes, they can tell).

How then, can you effectively obtain backlinks to help boost your search rankings? Here are my specific Pareto SEO methods for achieving this. Note that these are listed approximately in order of importance, so if you're searching for the 4% solution (the top 20% of the top 20%), just do the first one or two.

1. **List your web site in directory sites, particularly local directories.** Many people claim that "web directories are dead". In one of their illustrious algorithm updates in 2012, Google removed hundreds of web directory listing sites from their database. The fact that they did this proves that certain directories were providing link benefits, and a number of them still operate. These sites require manual submission of your web site, and there is no guarantee they will include your site. Local directories in particular have become more and more important due to the growth of "local search", and Google's emphasis of local in their algorithm.

   Since there are so many directory sites out there, how do you know which ones are worth your time? Remember, the goal here is to apply the 20% rule in order to maximize results with minimal effort. In that vein, here are the top local search listing sites that matter for our purposes. In SEO parlance, profiles on these sites are called "citations".

   Please note that this list in particular is subject to frequent change, and the second half of the list in particular would spark heated conversation if this topic was broached among a gathering of SEO nerds. These are the sites that my research and testing have proven to be most effective over the course of the past year and a half or so.

   - Google Places – Claim your own Google Places listing LAST, after creating local citations in other places (http://www.google.com/business/placesforbusiness/)
   - Yahoo Local (https://smallbusiness.yahoo.com/local-listings/)
   - Bing Places (https://www.bingplaces.com/dashboard)
   - Yelp (https://biz.yelp.com/support)
   - Thumbtack – professional services directory, not available in all states (https://www.thumbtack.com/welcome/)
   - PTINDirectory.com – the one tax professional directory that was built via email spamming of the IRS PTIN list that actually survived and has been accepted by Google as authoritative for our industry (http://www.ptindirectory.com/tax-preparer-registration.cfm)
   - Facebook page for your business (with your address, name, phone, keywords)
   - YellowPages.com
   - Manta.com
   - Cortera.com
   - MerchantCircle.com
   - HotFrog.com
   - Kudzu.com
   - Avvo.com (for lawyers only)

- Localeze.com

Additional directory tips:
- Google yourself, find existing online citations, and fix them.
- Citation lookup tool: http://www.moz.com/local
- Use the identical business name, address, phone number, and web site URL reference in all profiles. Be sure to include this exact same information, in the same format, on your own web site in multiple places (About page, footer, etc.)

2. **Submit your blog feed (the RSS feed URL we used for the blog broadcasts) to "blog aggregators".** These are sites that assemble blog entries from other blogs, providing links back to the original post. The top blog aggregators include sites such as Technorati.com, Alltop.com, Blogarama.com, and Liquida.com.

3. **Create infographics.** We're fortunate to be in an industry where numbers are our forte. This lends itself well to the creation of all sorts of pretty graphs, charts, and other statistical presentations. Since infographics are all the rage these days, we can leverage this to our backlink advantage. You can collect data of any variety you want (I like to repurpose Statistics of Income data, and IRS Collections Activity data), and feed it into a site like Piktochart.com to create free infographics. Then, seed these out to the world via Visual.ly, DailyInfoGraphic.com, AmazingInfoGraphics.com, OMGInfoGraphics.com, and, of course, Pinterest.com. At the same time, reach out to your professional network and offer them them the infographic to post on their site. With every posting, offer a custom text intro, and voila, you've got more backlinks.

4. **Donate to charity.** There are a slew of broke charities out there that have highly-ranked web sites. In exchange for a donation, many of these charities will acknowledge your donation on their own web site, and thus provide a link to your site. To find such charities, try searching for the following along with your geographical location or cause of interest:

    "donate to us"
    "contributors page"
    "sponsors page"
    allintitle: "contributors"
    allintitle: "sponsors"

5. **Participate in forums.** The Internet is awash with communities both big and small where online discussions about personal finance and business finance matters take place. These forums are usually free, and always have people coming to them asking tax and accounting questions. Answer these questions for people, and include a link to your site in the signature of your posts. This creates links for you, and also helps you establish credibility and authority in these communities, potentially leading to direct client engagements. While I have not received any direct client engagements because of it yet, I have been quite surprised by how many tax debtors and email leads I've received in the past month or so since I became active on a popular business opportunity and marketing forum online. Do a Google search for "personal finance forum" or similar keywords to find these sites online.

6. **Post Craigslist ads.** This may be the most surprising one on the list, but it should not be neglected. Craigslist is one of the most popular web sites in America, and ads DO get indexed by Google as long as the ads stay up for a while. The key to using Craigslist is two-fold:

   - Write one ad that you never delete, so it's "seasoned". Include a link in this ad to your site.
   - Create a different ad that you repost every 3 days, as is allowed by the Craigslist terms of service.

   Don't scoff at the idea of using Craigslist. This in particular is something that should be done by another staff member as part of their weekly duties, if you have staff. My largest ever single-fee tax resolution client (a $25,000 fee) came from a lowly Craigslist ad.

Be Published

We already discussed this heavily in the setup steps, but the entire purpose of building our new lead generation site on a blogging platform was to take advantage of the SEO power of publishing frequent educational articles on your own site. **Regularly publishing new articles on your own blog is the single most important SEO factor on your web site itself.** Refer back to the editorial calendar step in the lead gen site mechanics process for further information on this.

Article Marketing

A common misconception is that article marketing is about getting links from the article directories. False! Utilizing article directories is actually about syndicating your content. The link juice from article marketing comes from bloggers and ezine publishers using your articles on their sites — that's where the links come from.

A couple other article tips:

1. Always publish your content on your own site first so that you get the author credit, then syndicate it.
2. The so-called "duplicate content penalty" as most people think of it doesn't exist. Write an original article, post it to your blog, get it indexed, upload it to article directory, you'll be fine.
3. The only article directories worth submitting to are EzineArticles.com and GoArticles.com. This is that minimization we're seeking. GoArticles is a distant second, and true minimization only uses EzineArticles.com.
4. Write readable articles for humans, not search engines.
5. Don't "spin" articles. They're unreadable, spammy, and don't contribute anything to the world.
6. Write longer articles, more people will use them in syndication. Shoot for 1,000 to 1,200 words for most articles.

7. Treat your resource box as the last paragraph of your article. Make any links back to your site flow naturally with the text.

Guest Blogging

Writing blog posts on other people's quality, authoritative blogs can be highly effective. It's the exact same thing as posting an article in an article directory, and then having that article show up on somebody else's site. The difference is that you're actively seeking out these opportunities.

One guest post I wrote on one highly read blog was solely responsible for the entire ranking of one of my authority sites for almost a year, until other things kicked in and started carrying the weight as well.

Using your professional network, find other professionals with web sites for whom you can write guest blog posts for, and include a link or two to your own web site in that article that you contribute.

To find other places to guest post, do Google searches for:

- "KEYWORD" "guest bloggers"
- "KEYWORD" "guest bloggers wanted"
- "KEYWORD" "submit guest post"
- "KEYWORD" "submit a guest post"
- "KEYWORD" "write for us"

Press Coverage

1. Write press releases and distribute them on sites such as PRLog.com. Do a Google search for "press release distribution" to find other sites to post press releases on if you wish, but PRLog.com is the only one I ever use, as it is the 800 lb gorilla for this sort of thing online.

2. Register with Help A Report Out (HARO) at http://www.helpareporter.com/sources. Major media outlets use the HARO service to find expert sources to quote in their stories. This could be you, as well as get you powerful links from very high profile web sites. When you sign up for HARO, you'll get three emails every day with requests from reporters for certain criteria. Don't sleep on these: One mention in a major news story can itself provide a major boost to your search engine ranking. The HARO system can be quite unfriendly to use, but it can be worthwhile for a while.

Video

It's impossible to ignore the place which video holds on the Internet today. There are dozens of video sites online, but there's only really one that matters: YouTube.

YouTube is super powerful for getting direct traffic, and also for getting you ranked highly on

Google directly. It is NOT necessary to create backlinks to your YouTube videos. Make videos for your 10 or 20 long tail keywords, and let the videos stand on their own two feet. Always place your target URL at the beginning of the description box for the video, and provide a detailed description (remember…we need text!).

In your videos, display the URL itself, and directly tell people to click or visit. This will also drive traffic. Never forget your call to action!

Additional YouTube tips:

1. Place your long tail keyword in the description field formatted in three ways: the phrase, "the phrase" (in quotes), [the phrase] (in brackets).
2. Add a transcript to the video. This is a relatively new feature. That text can be of big help to SEO.
3. Make sure your YouTube channel is named after your primary keywords.
4. Get **views** to the video to rank it better. Embed the video on blogs, social media, etc.

Be Engaged

Social media engagement is the latest addition to my Pareto SEO strategy. I have largely attempted to ignore social media for years, but it's importance in Google's algorithm has grown to the point where it just cannot be ignored. Google will not tell us exactly how important social signals are in their algorithm, but various SEO experts peg it at around 10% to 20%.

The addition of social media engagement to my Pareto SEO strategy meant that other things had to be taken off the list. If you're curious as to what was removed, it was all from the "Be Listed" section (primarily "Web 2.0 properties" and social bookmarking sites). The growth of social media's significance in SEO largely has to do with the sharing of links by social media users. Therefore, *social media engagement is essentially a link building strategy*, and I treat it as such, even though it now has it's own special section here.

When it comes to social media engagement, the Pareto Principle applies further here. While there are a growing number of social media sites, only the big ones really matter, and I'm sure I don't even need to list them – you already know what they are. But here they are, in descending order of user base size:

- Facebook
- Twitter
- LinkedIn
- Pinterest
- Google+

Facebook, Twitter, and Google+ all permit essentially the same strategy. Pinterest is briefly covered under the infographic creation section of "Be Listed", and LinkedIn is an animal unto itself. Under the 20% rule, we're really only going to pay attention to Facebook, Twitter, and Google+.

Facebook, Twitter, Google+

These big three social media sites are all about sharing information across your fans, followers, and circles (I'll use Twitter's *follower* vernacular from here on out).

On Facebook, be sure to conduct all your business activity from a Facebook page, not your personal profile. Facebook has specific page types for local small businesses. You can ask clients and prospects to "like" your page, and run special offers on your Facebook page in order to encourage clients to "like" your page and go to it occasionally. Not that I suggest it, but you can also run Facebook ad campaigns to collect "likes".

You obtain Twitter followers in much the same way. Twitter has a new advertising platform that will let you run "promoted tweets", but organic is the best approach. Ask prospects, clients, and web site visitors to follow you on Twitter to obtain tax updates and special offers. An excellent way to attract Twitter followers is by searching for various tax-related hashtags, such as #tax, and answering tax questions that people post on the twitter stream. Follow other local small businesses as well.

For Google+, Google makes it easy to start filling your circles: Just give them access to your email contact list. While Twitter and Facebook also support this function, the large number of Gmail users makes this particularly attractive on Google+, since you know that Google will let *their* emails get through to Gmail users.

Now, what about the engagement part?

Social media doesn't need to be an extensive part of your day. And, quite frankly, it shouldn't be. Let's look at what you should do on a daily basis to engage with people on Twitter, Facebook, and G+.

First, spend about 5 minutes every day looking at your feed on each service. These are the streams of informatio being entered by the people you follow.

The key to success on social media is to be part of the conversation – not just a marketing piece. Re-tweet some of the other people's stuff if it's good, reply to other people's comments, and post your own insights.

What on Earth should you post? Basic stuff works amazingly well: Tax deduction tips, tax deadlines, collections advice. Always post links to your new blog posts, article directory submissions, press releases, guests posts, etc. (see how this is starting to come full circle?)

Encourage people to ask you tax questions. Use the search feature to LOOK for people asking tax questions. Use search terms such as "IRS" and "tax question" to find people that are looking for questions that YOU can answer in regards to taxes.

Don't spend more than 10 or 15 minutes a day doing all this for each service. Most days, I'm on Twitter for 2 minutes or less. There really is no reason to spend more time on there than that.

Just like any other marketing vehicle, using social media effectively for growing your tax practice has to do with building the KLT factor. KLT stands for "know, like, trust." People do business with people that they know, that they like, and that they trust, and engaging with them via social media in a non-threatening and non-salesman environment is an important element for actually gaining their business.

It's easy to get lost in the social media game – but there's no need to do that. There's also no need to avoid being on these sites, and by making it an integrated (yet short) part of your overall and consistent marketing plan you are taking advantage of one of the most powerful tools for engaging directly with prospects that exists today. As you engage with other users, your fans/followers/circles will grow, and *people will share with other people* the links and other content you post.

Paid Traffic

The entire point of setting our new lead generation web site up on a WordPress blog was to take advantage of the incredible power of search engines to deliver us FREE traffic. Under this model, the time (or money) you invest in creating and maintaining your lead generation site(s) is a direct investment in marketing, and the ROI can be astronomical.

Now of course the leads we get from our free traffic aren't actually free. There is the cost of setting up and maintaining the site. But, now that you have it, there are additional ways to leverage your existing investment in that site in order to grow your lead base even faster. Considering the fact that search engine optimization efforts typically take between three and six months in order to see real results, the use of paid traffic generation methods can accelerate the process of obtaining a return on our investment into this lead generation site.

Facebook Ads

Over the course of the past year, I have done a ton of Facebook ad testing, spending over $8,000 across a variety of test campaigns. I even purchased two "get rich quick online" courses that teach Facebook advertising, and tested each of them (that was a waste of money!).

Facebook is fairly attractive as an advertising platform for a number of reasons, including:

- The sheer number of Americans that have a Facebook account and check it regularly.
- The ability to very clearly target your Facebook ads to specific demographics and geographics.
- Minimum daily ad budget of only $1 per campaign.

Facebook allows you to have a variety of different objectives for your campaign, and various ways of displaying ads. In general, you can choose to keep your Facebook traffic on Facebook, or send it to your own website. Most of the information that you'll find online from "Internet marketing gurus", including inside some rather expensive courses, will teach you to maximize the number of "likes" that you get to your Facebook page.

My own live tests of Facebook advertising tactics have been spread across many different subjects. **The results of my testing have demonstrated unequivocally that Facebook page likes are utterly worthless.**

I realize that is quite a bold statement to make in this current business environment where social media is the beloved princess, so please hear me out. Facebook wants you to keep your traffic on Facebook itself, since it's in their own best interest to keep as many people on their site for as long as possible each day. Due to this, Facebook actually rewards you with a lower Cost Per Click (CPC) on your ads if they are directed at a Facebook page, as well as less hassle with getting your ads approved by their reviewers. What I've discovered, however, is that your **Facebook page fans don't actually engage with you in the future**.

The way it's supposed to work is that somebody "likes" your page, and then whenever you post on that page, all your fans see your new posts in their News Feed. However, what actually happens is that somewhere around 5% of your fans will actually see your posts in their News Feed, unless you pay Facebook additional money via their "Boost Your Post" feature.

In other words, Facebook charges you a click fee to get the page like, and then wants you to pay additional fees to get your posts seen by people that already liked your page. This is the fundamental problem with building a Facebook page. The vast majority of your fans will never actually see your page again. This is true for almost all business pages on Facebook, since most of us will never get enough fans to our page to create the natural avalanche effect that social media relies upon in terms of sharing and appearing more relevant (this is called "going viral").

Facebook does not tell us how many fans you need in order for the natural increase in sharing and News Feed viewership to kick in, but I've read various studies suggesting it's somewhere between 10,000 and 500,000. Not only is that a huge spread of uncertainty, but even the biggest tax and accounting firms in the world barely hit those kinds of numbers.

KPMG, for example, has 21,377 page fans. By way of comparison, the official page for the 2012 Colorado recreational marijuana legalization effort has 27,426 page likes, and the cult movie classic "Rocky Horror Picture Show" has over 7640,000. Heck, even the AICPA has less than 9,000 page likes.

This analysis should explain why major Fortune 500 brands have literally been abandoning their Facebook page advertising efforts. General Motors, for example, made big news in late 2013 when they announced that they would stop spending money on ALL of their paid social media advertising, citing an absolute inability to peg vehicle sales to the marketing medium. A Google search will reveal additional companies that have done the same thing.

Another thing I noticed while doing this Facebook ad testing was the fact that the major Internet marketing "gurus", some of whom taught the strategy of getting page likes through various means, did not themselves use this strategy. If you have their ads displayed to you, which simply takes "liking" a few pages on your own, you'll see that they ALL actually drive traffic to their own web sites. In this way, **they are treating Facebook the same way you would Google Adwords.**

While you will pay a higher CPC for sending your clicks to a site other than a Facebook page, the value of that traffic is higher. It is lost on many people that Facebook "likes" are NOT leads. They're not even opt-ins. I'd much rather have somebody sign up for my email newsletter on my tax practice web site, then email them weekly. At least then I know that they'll receive the message, since well over ¾ of all Internet users still consider their email inbox the hub of their online activity (the number varies by study, but all are over 75%).

What about directing your Facebook ad clicks to a special tab on your Facebook page that contains the email signup? This is another heavily touted strategy amongst the online "gurus". However, in my testing of this strategy, I discovered that people simply click the "like" button that appears above your landing page, and very, very few actually provide their email address or other information.

In a very brief (and rather expensive) test of this for trying to get tax resolution leads, I got a bunch of new "likes" to my tax practice page, but not a single actual lead that I could follow up with.

Even big companies like Monster and Outbrain have figured out what I'm referring to here. I'm also seeing a ton of TurboTax ads right now, and they all direct to Intuit's own web site, not their Facebook page. There is a strong take away from this that you can apply in your own practice.

So, the generic suggestion for running Facebook ads is to configure your campaigns like this:

1. Run one ad variation per campaign, with multiple images (creating multiple ad variations, but varying only because of the image).

2. Set your demographic targeting to your local area. Creating separate ad groups for different cities, even if they are close together. For example, if you're in Seattle, create different Facebook ad groups for Kent, Renton, Tacoma, Everett, etc.

3. If you're advertising to get business clients, use the advanced targeting feature to select small business owners. This will show your ads only to people that have indicated in their profiles that they are small business owners or self-employed.

4. Don't neglect the age, marital status, and gender realities of your ideal clients.

5. Start your campaigns at $5 to $10 daily, and run for at least a week.

6. Set your ads to manually bid for clicks. I highly suggest avoiding the feature where Facebook will optimize your bidding automatically for you. Set your initial manual bid somewhere near the high end of the range that Facebook suggests to you, but not the absolute maximum. If Facebook suggests to me a range of 39 to 58 cents, I'll put it at 50 cents to start.

7. Set all ad clicks to go to an appropriate lead generation site. If you're running tax planning ads, send them to your new tax planning lead generation site you created using the 13-step process in this manual.

Here is one example Facebook ad that I was running to gather attendees on a webinar in late 2013:

Ad Preview   Edit Creative   Targeting

Owe The IRS $50k Or More?
freetaxwebinar.com

Free online tax debt relief workshop shows you how to protect assets from the IRS.

View on Right Hand Side
Create a Similar Ad

Potential Audience for this ad: 4,400,000 people
- Location: United States
- Age: 30 and older
- Interests: small business or #Republican Party (United States)
- Education Level: College grad
- Relationship Status: Married
- Language: English (Pirate) or English (US)
- on Right column on desktop computers

Suggested Bid: $0.18 - 0.34 USD

You'll notice that I was targeting a pretty wide audience with this particular ad. I was not using an geographical targeting, and was targeting two extremely wide interests. Note that I would run a slightly different ad at the same time, targeting Democratic Party small business owners, with slightly different wording that did not mention asset protection, but rather income protection (there are valid survey-based reasons for this party distinction, but that is beyond the scope of this manual).

If you're interested in the results for this ad, it resulted in 46 clicks, at an average cost of 61 cents per click. I only ran the ad for a few days to get some people on the webinar, and spent a total of $28.43 on this particular ad to get a few leads into my tax debt resolution sales funnel.

Running this sort of an ad on a continual basis, and directing them to a webinar replay that looks live is an effective online lead generation strategy. A version of this ad also directs to my most basic online lead capture page, and the ad simply says, "Learn 5 questions to ask to protect yourself from tax resolution predators," with the headline changed from referencing $50,000 to instead referencing $15,000. Facebook ads have to be short, and that one is a bit aggressive, but the right person is responsive to that message.

One final thought on Facebook ads. Facebook allows you to define "Custom Audiences", based on email or telephone lists. Inside the Facebook ads platform, on the left side, select audiences:

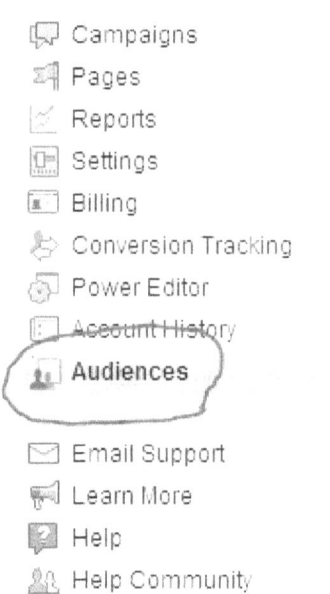

That takes you to the listing page of Custom Audiences. In the upper right corner, select the green "Create Audience" button to be taken to the custom audience editor. In the editor, you will upload a CSV file containing only email addresses OR phone numbers. Name and save the custom audience, and then in the future when you create new Facebook ads, you can select the custom audience to use, rather than selecting any of the other demographic targeting options.

What's the value of custom audiences?

Let's say that you've created new lead generation site using the 13-step method in this manual in order to attract new high net worth tax planning and wealth management clients (a potential rare example of a dual-purpose lead gen site, since the two services are closely connected).

At the same time, you've purchased a list of high net worth investors from a list broker, such as InfoUSA. You could then run this list through an email append service, which will return a smaller list of the same people with email addresses added (InfoUSA won't sell you email addresses).

Then, you can remove everything except the email address column in Excel, save the file as a CSV, and import this to a Faceook custom audience. Lastly, you create an ad specifically targeting that custom audience, with a compelling ad. A quick example off the top of my head might be something like:

Headline: Paying too much tax?
Ad body: Free report reveals 8 tax saving strategies you're probably missing.

...then they click to your lead generation page and are presented with the special report.

This ad will only show to the people from the email list that you uploaded. It probably won't be very many people, but it will be highly targeted.

You can use this same strategy to advertise tax debt resolution by creating custom audiences using tax lien lists based on phone numbers, instead of telemarketing to them. See http://TaxLiensHQ.net to obtain tax lien lists for advertising tax resolution, unfiled tax return preparation, and business bookkeeping services in particular using this strategy.

For tax return preparation, you can use this same method to target new homeowners that recently moved to your city, or new business owners. New business registration lists and new movers lists are two of the most commonly available and easy to find lists available. The USPS service at http://Click2Mail.com not only offers cheap print and postage services, but also offers these kinds of common mailing lists at fairly cheap rates.

Did you create a specialty niche lead generation site, targeted to a specific group of people? This strategy works for them, also. Let's say you created a lead gen site targeting the tax advising needs of real estate investors. You can obtain an _absentee owners list_ from a local source (tip: try a title company), then run an email or phone append on that list, and then create a custom audience in Facebook to target ads just to them.

Hopefully you see the vast potential of Facebook ads for driving traffic to multiple lead capture web site that you create using this manual. I would encourage you to set aside a test budget of at least several hundred dollars per month to test your own ad ideas.

Resources

Additional Example Lead Generation Sites

These are just a couple of my lead generation sites. I have others that I'm not mentioning here, of course, and these sites may well change by the time some readers see this. But regardless, I thought I'd share two additional examples so you could see alternate approaches.

Generic, keyword-based feeder lead gen site: http://irsdebthelphq.com/

Extremely basic lead generation site with no blog, used to gather direct mail postcard responses: http://irsfreshstart.com/

My primary tax firm web site, woefully out of date: http://taxhelphq.com

Sample Emails

You are welcome to use any of these sample emails for your own lead generation sites. You may wish to edit them for your own personality and "voice", of course. The only exception is the use of my *Taxing Times*™ trademark. If you use any of the emails referencing *Taxing Times*™, please create your own name for your email newsletter and use that.

Full welcome email from the example site in this manual:

Subject: The solution to your IRS back tax problem...

Body:

You've taken a great first step towards resolving your IRS back tax problems!

Our firm works with taxpayers across the country, and we recognize that every tax situation is unique. We are here to eliminate the threat and worry caused by the IRS Collections division in your life.

As promised, here is the special report you requested, "5 Questions To Ask Any Tax Resolution Firm Before Paying Them A Dime":

http://irsbacktaxproblemhelp.com/welcome

We look forward to working with you to resolve your tax situation. Regardless of whether you are actively looking for representation or just looking at your options, we urge you to give us a call at _____ to discuss your situation with one of our licensed tax professionals.

Sincerely,

_____

Sample welcome email from my own tax firm site. If you use this sort of approach, please change the name of the newsletter to your own, of course – I'm not relinquishing the *Taxing Times*™ name anytime soon. ☺

Subject: Welcome to the Taxing Times™ newsletter!

Body:

==
Taxing Times™ Email Newsletter
Brought to you by TaxHelpHQ.com
==

Thank you for subscribing to the Taxing Times™ newsletter!

Every week, you will receive up to date news regarding America's tax situation, including strategic advice for helping you reduce your own tax bill.

In addition, I'll share with you my personal take on the economy and the situation in Congress, and how it impacts your family and your business.

Since many readers subscribe to this newsletter because of an existing tax debt, you will find attached a free special report detailing the "5 Questions To Ask Any Tax Resolution Firm Before Paying Them A Dime".

If you are considering hiring professional tax representation, I highly encourage you to read this report and heed the advice it contains before hiring ANY company in order to avoid becoming a victim of an unethical tax resolution firm or straight up fraud, which runs rampant in the tax resolution industry.

I look forward to having you on board, and providing you with the information you need to reduce your tax bill and have a more prosperous personal economy!

Sincerely,

Jassen Bowman, EA
TaxHelpHQ.com

Sample Tax Resolution Follow Message #1

Note: I suggest setting your follow up messages to be sent 2-3 days apart for the first several messages, then change to a weekly follow up schedule thereafter.

Subject: IRS issues? First, stop the bleeding.

Body:

When you owe the IRS money, life can be pretty miserable. If you have already experienced wage garnishments, bank account levies, or any of the other nasty actions that the government can take against you, then you already know what I'm talking about.

This newsletter is about more than just resolving tax problems, but since that is most likely brought you here, I want to start right off the bat with a bit of tax advice that applies to just about everybody:

In order to get on the road to financial recovery, the first priority is to either STOP or PREVENT the overly aggressive collections tactics used by the IRS.

In order to protect yourself from wage garnishments and bank accounts funds from mysteriously disappearing, you have to get into some sort of protected status. There are a number of ways to do this, but the two most common are:

1. File an appeal that provides such protection, or

2. Enter into direct negotiations for a final resolution.

With the right appeal filed at the right time (these have narrow windows of opportunity attached to them), or applying for the right IRS settlement program that you meet the qualifications for, you can PREVENT the IRS from taking nasty collections action against you.

For example, filing a Collection Due Process appeal within 30 days of receiving a "Final Notice of Intent to Levy" (look for "Letter 1058" in the upper right or lower right corner of the notice) can get you several months of protection.

Similarly, filing a request for a payment plan or filing an application for an Offer in Compromise also gives you specific legal protections from aggressive IRS collection tactics.

We will cover specific tax resolution topics in future issues of this newsletter, and you can also find articles, tools, calculators, and helpful resources on our web site at http://www.taxhelphq.com.

Sincerely,

Jassen Bowman, EA
TaxHelpHQ.com

Sample Tax Resolution Follow Up Message #2

Subject: Conducting research before hiring a tax resolution firm

Body:

When it comes to something as important as resolving your tax liabilities, it is important to conduct research on the tax resolution firm(s) you are considering before agreeing to purchase their services.

What sort of things should somebody do as part of conducting their "due diligence"?

First of all, visit the Better Business Bureau at www.bbb.com and look for any complaints or outstanding issues that they have with clients.

Second, you may actually want to turn to an unlikely source for information on certain companies: Your IRS Revenue Officer. Revenue Officers will not provide an unbiased opinion, of course, and many of them will even tell you not to secure representation (which is a violation of IRS policies for them to say, but they still do it). However, your RO has probably worked with most of the large, national tax resolution firms and can give you their personal opinion on the firm if you ask.

Third, before signing a contract for taxpayer representation, be sure to confirm that the firm that will provide your representation will assign your case to a licensed representative. You should be guaranteed that your representative is a licensed attorney, licensed certified public, accountant, or a licensed Enrolled Agent, before you sign any contract. The IRS will not allow non-licensed representatives to negotiate for a taxpayer, but you would be surprised at how often large firms have unlicensed assistants doing the actual IRS negotiation.

Fourth, be sure to ask if the individual selling you the tax resolution service if they have ever been involved in actual IRS or state tax negotiations. Many times you will get a delayed answer because that answer is "no." Be weary of salespersons that will base how they can help you from a sales script. Any case-experienced salesperson should be able to walk you through the case proceedings from start to finish. On top of that, it is *illegal* for an unlicensed person to give you tax advice or even offer to sell you tax services.

Understand that hiring a representative to negotiate on your behalf is not a guarantee that your case will be resolved. You will need to work closely with your representative to ensure that your best interests are always held in high regard. Although your representative should do nearly all of the interaction with the taxing authorities, your participation with your representative is vital to the resolution process.

It is very important for you to keep in mind that most of the time when you are speaking with a tax resolution firm, you are speaking to a commissioned sales rep on the phone. These sales reps usually have zero actual tax experience, and much of what they tell you may have been passed to them from OTHER untrained personnel. This is important to understand because it is not uncommon for these salespeople to give blatantly incorrect information to people simply so they can close a sale.

Armed with these tips, you should be better positioned to make a wise decision regarding hiring professional tax services.

Sincerely,

Jassen Bowman, EA
TaxHelpHQ.com

Sample Tax Resolution Follow Up Message #3

Subject: How the IRS works collections cases

Body:

When a taxpayer owes money to the IRS, they enter the IRS Collections system. The IRS has a very detailed process that they are required by law to follow when it comes to collecting tax debts. Knowing a little bit about how this system works and how IRS collections personnel are required to act can be very beneficial to you.

There are two distinct collections units within the IRS. The first is the Automated Collection System (ACS), which consists of computerized lien filings, automated send out of bills and notices on set intervals, and the call center agents that perform basic collections functions. It is important to understand that the people you're talking to on the phone at ACS are generally not very highly trained individuals, and have very limited authority.

They are trained to do their jobs, and that's really about it. In fact, speaking with ACS representatives is on par with speaking to a customer service representative at your cell phone provider, and can be equally as frustrating if you get somebody that just can't wait to go home for the day.

The other distinct collection unit within the IRS is the Collection Field function. Field agents, called Revenue Officers, are located in cities and towns across the country. Rural Revenue Officers may actually work from home and have a field territory covering hundreds of miles, while thousands of agents in big cities have extremely small territories and may hardly ever leave their Federal Building.

Revenue Officers are required to do many things in order to "resolve" a tax liability placed under their control. They are required, by law and regulation, to collection certain information, verify things through whatever means available, and close out cases. Over the course of the past year and a half or so, I have personally noticed a significantly reduced emphasis on simply reducing the number of open cases, and instead increasing cash collections through whatever means necessary.

In order to demonstrate to IRS management that they are doing their jobs properly, here are some of the biggest actions that Revenue Officers are required to perform (and document in their files):

--Make sure you've filed every past tax return you should have (and if not, make you do so)

--Verify that you are making payments on time and in full for any new taxes you have come up, such as employment taxes or estimated tax payments (and if you're not, making sure that you do)

--Collect detailed financial information from you concerning your income, expenses, assets, and other debts

--Based on that financial information, determine sources of money from which the government can collect on the tax debt (this can include forcing you to apply for loans against property with equity or tapping into retirement accounts)

--Place you into whatever program you qualify for in order to address the tax liability, such as a monthly payment plan, reduced settlement, or even giving you a grace period of a year or two in which they close your case (but you still owe the debt, and it grows)

--Make sure you don't accumulate any new tax debts

--Physically visit your home or business at least once in order to determine if you're hiding anything (free and clear Hummer sitting in the barn -- it's happened)

--If you are a business and owe employment taxes, determine whom to assess the Trust Fund Recovery Penalty against on a personal level, and do so

--If you are not meeting deadlines or they believe you are stalling, hiding money, or have an ability to make payments and you're simply not, then to issue levies and take money from your bank account, paycheck, customers, etc.

All IRS collections employees keep meticulous notes whenever they talk to anybody (hint: so should you!). It's not uncommon for an IRS Collections file to be hundreds of pages of material, even for what might seem like a relatively small case.

All in all, don't forget that the IRS Collections division has one priority: To collect money. Hopefully, having a little bit better understanding of how they work cases will help you in resolving your IRS matters if you choose to do so on your own.

Sample Tax Resolution Follow Message #4

Subject: Watch your back...

Body:

There's an old joke about lawyers: 99% of attorneys give the rest a bad name.

Well, I have almost identical feelings about tax resolution sales guys.

When it comes to tax resolution sales people, I have one very important word of wisdom:

Watch your back!

The tax resolution world is filled with unlicensed, commissioned salespeople. I've worked with quite a few of these guys, especially from the bigger firms that are based in Colorado.

Not only is it *illegal* for unlicensed people to solicit licensed tax services, but I wouldn't trust most of these guys to sell me a Kleenex. Many of them are just straight up worse than used car salesman.

Most tax resolution salesmen have ZERO formal training in taxation, in any way. The ones that do have training are often barely trained enough to speak some lingo and identify a few common scenarios where a particular IRS program *might* be a possibility for a customer.

It's not uncommon for these salespeople to straight up LIE to people. Here are common examples of the lies that I heard being told on the phone at a firm I used to work at:

-interest charges can be eliminated
-penalty reductions are guaranteed
-everybody is eligible to settle for "pennies on the dollar"
-your case will get assigned to a new, "nicer" Revenue Officer
-your bank accounts will get drained by the IRS in 10 days if you don't hire a representative

Not only this, but I've heard sales guys verbally abusing prospective clients....and get away with it. Shouting, swearing, and threatening IRS actions that can't happen, just to scare people into signing a check.

In order to avoid these lies and verbal abuse, I have one fundamental rule that I encourage everybody with tax problems to follow:

===
Don't take tax advice from anybody that isn't licensed.
===

Licensed tax professionals, such as attorneys, CPA's, and Enrolled Agents (licensed directly by the US Treasury) are the most most knowledgeable tax professionals in America, and are the only people that can legally represent you as your Power of Attorney.

By only speaking with a licensed tax professional, you at least have some minimal guarantee of competency and the requirement by that individual to uphold a higher ethical standard.

Bottom line: Choose your counsel wisely, especially when it comes to something as critical as your tax and financial life.

Sincerely,

Jassen Bowman, EA

Sample Report

TaxMarketingHQ.com

Special Report: "5 Questions To Ask Any Tax Resolution Firm Before Paying Them A Dime"

When it comes to something as important as resolving your tax liabilities, it is important to conduct research on the tax resolution firm(s) you are considering before agreeing to purchase their services.

What sort of things should somebody do as part of conducting their "due diligence"?

Question #1: Are you licensed to be providing me tax advice?

Many tax resolution firms use unlicensed sales personnel to sell their services. These sales people do not possess the professional knowledge to be advising you on your tax matters, nor are they legally allowed to do so. The only people that can advise you on tax matters are Enrolled Agents (EA), Certified Public Accountants (CPA), and attorneys. Ask the person you're speaking to whether they are licensed. If they say anything other than EA, CPA, or attorney, then they are not licensed.

Some sales people have even been known to make up something or just give you their title at their firm ("Senior Tax Analyst"). Several people have received criminal convictions for this misrepresentation, but it still occurs.

Question #2: What is your BBB rating?

Ask the company what their BBB rating is, and then verify it. Do a Google search for the name of the company plus the words "better business bureau". This should take you directly to their BBB record in most cases, and you can see the rating, plus how long they've been in business and how many complaints they have had.

Question #3: Are you the actual person that will be representing me?

Third, before signing a contract for taxpayer representation, be sure to confirm that the firm that will provide your representation will assign your case to a licensed representative. You should be guaranteed that your representative is a licensed EA, CPA, or attorney, even if it's somebody else in the firm other than the licensed person you're already speaking to. The IRS will not allow non-licensed representatives to negotiate for a taxpayer, but you would be surprised at how often large firms have unlicensed assistants doing the actual IRS negotiation. Before you sign a contract or send money, make sure you see the IRS Form 2848, Power of Attorney, which lists the name(s) of the people actually representing you.

Question #4: Have you ever actually been involved in negotiating tax resolutions?

In other words, has the person you are speaking to actually worked on tax cases as a representative. It's one thing to be licensed, quite another to have actual case experience or not.

Because the government is cracking down on sales practices, some sales closers have actually taken the Enrolled Agent exam and become licensed. This is better than not being licensed, of course, but it still does not make them qualified to offer tax advice regarding your IRS debt if they have no actual case experience. Any case-experienced, licensed salesperson should be able to walk you through the case proceedings from start to finish.

Question #5: What precisely does the fee you are quoting me include?

The tax resolution is notorious for rebilling clients for work that either doesn't need to be done, was excessively overbilled for originally, or that should have been included in the your orginal fee quote.

Many tax resolution firms operate on a "flat fee" basis. In theory, the fee they quote you should include EVERYTHING necessary to resolve your case. Make sure that fee includes some of these necessary actions:

- All Appeals filings
- Full negotiation of resolution
- Preparation of any missing tax returns
- Removal of any existing levies or wage garnishments
- Representation for all tax types, including state taxes if needed
- For business owners, make sure you are covered for Trust Fund Recovery Penalty
- representation. This is critical to prevent getting personally stuck with your business tax bill.
- Application for a penalty abatement if you meet "reasonable cause criteria".

If the tax firm you are speaking to works on a retainer basis with hourly fees, rather than a flat fee, be sure to see a schedule of service fees, and get a copy of their billing policy.

Ask for an estimate of what the total charges will be, and get that in writing.

Understand that hiring a representative to negotiate on your behalf is not a guarantee that your case will be resolved. You will need to work closely with your representative to ensure that your best interests are always held in high regard. Although your representative should do nearly all of the interaction with the taxing authorities, your participation with your representative is vital to the resolution process, so be sure you select somebody that you are going to be able to work with without personality conflicts.

Lastly, be sure that anything and everything you discuss with a tax resolution firm, such as fees, covered services, responsibilities, deadlines, etc., are all in WRITING. Don't sign a contract, and definitely don't give them your credit card number without seeing everything in writing first.

Armed with these questions, you should be better positioned to make a wise decision regarding hiring professional tax services.

[CALL TO ACTION GOES HERE!!!]

Conclusion

The Internet is one of the most powerful marketing mediums ever created. Properly used, it can fuel massive growth in any business. In the Information Age, informed consumers spend more time than ever researching the products and services that they purchase, and they often do extensive online searching to learn about specific services and service providers. **You need to be online in order for them to have a chance of finding you.**

Whether you choose to implement the strategy in this manual yourself, or outsource the whole process to an assistant, a high school kid, or another company, I hope that you have taken the time to at least read this manual and grasp what's contained. Having read this manual will put you light years ahead of your peers when you're having the conversation with a web design or SEO company, for example.

Above all else, I want to encourage you to take action. There are potential clients out there right now searching online for your services, and it's up to you to put the systems in place to allow them to find and hire you.

To learn about additional marketing courses, practice management checklists, and other tools available from Jassen Bowman, please visit http://taxmarketinghq.com/products-services/.

Free Bonus

This book is really just the beginning of your journey. In order to support you in your efforts at growing your tax practice, we created a **membership website** that has additional training and resources to help you build your tax resolution practice.

The great news is that access to this site is 100% free. To get access, go to:

www.TaxMarketingHQ.com/bonus

Here is what you'll receive:

- A comprehensive 6-hour video series that introduces you to the essentials of starting and growing a tax resolution practice, including the fundamentals of marketing, client intake, practice management, sales, and tax resolution case work.
- Detailed training on how to find your first tax resolution client.
- How to quote tax resolution fees.
- The world famous *One-Hour Per Day Marketing Plan*.
- Access to complimentary CE/CPE webinars on IRS Collections topics.
- Additional links, resources, and bonuses from the book.
- A few surprises along the way.

You can access everything at:

https://TaxMarketingHQ.com/bonus

Please note that this offer is subject to change or substitution at any time.